Digital Expressions

Creating Digital Art with Adobe® Photoshop® Elements

SUSAN TUTTLE

NORTH LIGHT BOOKS
Cincinnati, Ohio

.

14 13 12 11 10   5 4 3 2 1

DISTRIBUTED IN CANADA BY FRASER DIRECT
100 Armstrong Avenue
Georgetown, ON, Canada L7G 5S4
Tel: (905) 877-4411

DISTRIBUTED IN THE U.K. AND EUROPE BY DAVID & CHARLES
Brunel House, Newton Abbot, Devon, TQ12 4PU, England
Tel: (+44) 1626 323200, Fax: (+44) 1626 323319
Email: postmaster@davidandcharles.co.uk

DISTRIBUTED IN AUSTRALIA BY CAPRICORN LINK
P.O. Box 704, S. Windsor NSW, 2756 Australia
Tel: (02) 4577-3555

Library of Congress Cataloging in Publication Data

Tuttle, Susan
 Digital expressions : creating digital art with Adobe Photoshop elements / by Susan Tuttle. -- 1st ed.
     p. cm.
 Includes index.
 ISBN-13: 978-1-60061-454-5 (pbk. : alk. paper)
 ISBN-10: 1-60061-454-X (pbk. : alk. paper)
 1. Photography--Digital techniques. 2. Adobe Photoshop elements. 3. Digital art. I. Title.
 TR267.5.A3T97 2010
 006.6'96--dc22
                                        2009039935

www.fwmedia.com

EDITOR
Kristin Boys

DESIGNER
Geoff Raker

PRODUCTION COORDINATOR
Greg Nock

Cover image credits:
Image of woman: ©iStockphotos.com/mlenny
Image of butterfly: ©iStockphotos.com/ranzino

METRIC CONVERSION CHART

To convert	to	multiply by
Inches	Centimeters	2.54
Centimeters	Inches	0.4
Feet	Centimeters	30.5
Centimeters	Feet	0.03
Yards	Meters	0.9
Meters	Yards	1.1

ABOUT THE AUTHOR

I am indebted to Tonia Davenport and the North Light team for believing in me and my ideas a second time around. I thank you from the depths of my heart. Applause, applause to my editor, Kristin Boys, for her clear thinking, flexibility and ideas that helped shape the presentation of this book. Thank you to all those at North Light Books who have made the production of this publication possible; your talents continue to amaze me. For all of the artists who made contributions: your stellar work has greatly enhanced this book. Thank you, Jessica Theberge, my dear friend, for treating me to a photo session with you; working with your imagery is a gift. To my husband and children, thank you for your unending love, support, encouragement and inspiration.

For Grace, my guardian angel, whose whispers I hear on the wind.

A big thank you to you, the reader, for joining me here. I hope you will enjoy the book and find it helpful.

SUSAN TUTTLE resides in a small, rural town in Maine, with her two children and supportive husband. Her studio, although tiny, has a marvelous view of the woods, which provides countless moments of inspiration as she works. She enjoys immersing herself in a wide variety of artistic mediums, including digital art, photography, collage, assemblage and altered art. Susan has a passion for blogging, where she attempts to capture, through photographs and the written word, the beauty of all things simple and ordinary in her life. She explores abstract intuitive painting on huge canvases, often with bold colors and patterns. You can often find her at the town dump, collecting vintage discards, metal scraps, and old, dusty books, which she lovingly brings back to life in her art.

Susan has played the flute since the age of nine, and went on to further pursue her musical studies at Rutgers University's Mason Gross School of the Arts and the Boston Conservatory. She taught K–12 public school music over a span of ten years, in both the Greater Boston area and in Maine. After a life-altering car accident in 1996, which she amazingly survived and came away from practically unscathed, she began her journey of creating art in the visual realm. She embraced this newfound part of herself and recognized it as being a necessary component of her life, one that she needed in order to feel complete and whole. Susan strongly believes that the arts, in whatever form they take, are for everyone—not just an elite few—and that it is never too early or too late to make it a part of your life.

Susan's first book, *Exhibition 36*, was published by North Light Books in 2008. Her work can also be seen in a variety of North Light Books publications as well as in *Somerset Studio* and several Stampington & Company special publications.

Susan is teaching digital art classes both online through her blog and at art retreats. Visit her blog at www.ilkasattic.blogspot.com and her Web site at www.ilkasattic.com.

CONTENTS

6   Introduction

8   Essential Tools and Techniques

19   What You'll Need

---

20   # 1 Manipulating Images
Using techniques to alter one or two photos

22   WHISPERS Creating Vignettes With Color Fill Layers

26   THE JACKS Popping Areas of Color

30   UNBOUND Designing With Type

34   ST. AUGUSTINE Overlaying Texture

---

38   # 2 Painting & Drawing
Applying brushwork and filters to mimic traditional art

40   SWEET SLUMBER Making Drawings with Artistic Filters: Colored Pencil

42   SHINE LIGHT Making Drawings with Artistic Filters: Colored Pencil + Dry Brush

44   HARVEST Replicating the Look of Traditional Painting

50   VERUCA'S DREAM Painting with Color Fill Layers

56   AGLAOPE Painting a Photo

62

3 Pasting Pieces
Layering elements to create digital collages

64 MY FLEDGLING Merging Transparent Layers

68 EN POINTE Applying Filters: Invert and Poster Edges

72 HOPE AT ROCK BOTTOM Applying Filters: Photo and Lighting Effects

76 GO FREE Creating With Scrapbook Kits

80 SELF-PORTRAIT Creating a Self-Portrait Collage

84 WALTER'S BROKEN HEART Colorizing With the Brush Tool

90

4 Seamlessly Blending
Merging images to create montage art

92 CAN WE? Creating Custom Brushes

96 THE CHASE Producing Motion With Blur Effects

100 TRAVEL LIGHT Creating Shadows With the Burn Tool

106 JUST FAMILY STOPPING BY Replacing Parts of a Photo

110 BETWEEN WORLDS Adding a Gradient Fill Layer for Lighting Effects

114 WINTER Using Staged Photos

120

5 Altering Art
Incorporating traditional art into digital works

122 CURIOSITY Enhancing Original Art

126 CELIE Using Art as a Background

132 THE RHYTHM Deconstructing and Reconstructing Art

136 THE POWER OF PRAYER Blending Multiple Works of Art

140 Digital Showcase

142 Index

INTRODUCTION

The mixed-media art world is constantly expanding its range of mediums and techniques; artists are always pushing the envelope, searching for new ways to create, in order to satisfy their creative passions and curiosities, and present their audience of mixed-media enthusiasts with fresh approaches and ideas. Digital art created with the use of photo-editing software is quickly becoming a part of this circle, including digital collage and montage, photopainting and digitally altered "actual" art.

Many mixed-media artists and enthusiasts are intrigued and eager to create this type of art, but are often unsure of how to begin or don't know where to find appropriate resources, as there are few on this specific subject. For those who have some digital experience, there is often frustration over the fact that they cannot find more advanced, fresh ideas. There is a plethora of books on photo-editing software, but they are more about the "ins and outs" of programs as they pertain to correcting photographs. There are also numerous publications on the subject of digital scrapbooking, which provide a wealth of spectacular information to draw from. In creating this book, I have melded together my knowledge of and experience with digital art and mixed-media techniques, in hopes of creating the type of resource you are looking for.

In this book, you'll find 25 stepped-out digital art projects in the areas of photo-manipulation, digital collage and montage, digital painting and digital alteration of traditional pieces of art. Each project highlights a particular artistic digital technique or concept. I created the projects using Adobe Photoshop® Elements® 6.0, which is available for both Macs and PCs. It is important to note that these projects are compatible with both earlier and subsequent versions of Photoshop Elements. Readers who are using Adobe Photoshop (including Photoshop CS) will also find the projects to be compatible with their software (though the instructions may vary).

In addition to the projects, you'll also find a reference section of essential techniques and tools (starting on page 8), which you can refer to as you go through the book. The Digital Showcase gallery (on page 140) features a sampling of my more advanced work that combines some of the project techniques you'll learn. Finally, I've included a CD that contains images and custom brushes for your personal use. In fact, some of the images I've used in the projects; these images are indicated by the CD icon in the Sources for Project Artwork lists.

Gregory Haun, author of *Photoshop Collage Techniques* (Hayden Books, 1997), makes a poignant observation about digital art. He defines it as an art form that draws from traditional painting, photography, collage, montage and graphic design. Digital art combines facets of these types of art and manipulates them in new and interesting ways, some of which were not previously possible prior to photo-editing digital technology.

Keep in mind that there is no one way to do something. This is especially true when it comes to creating digital art with an image-editing program. As you experiment with this book and your software, you will find that there are several ways to approach the same task. That being said, use this book any way you see fit—replicate the projects, tweak them or use them as a springboard for your own unique ideas.

Jump in and have fun!
SUSAN

ESSENTIAL TOOLS AND TECHNIQUES

In this section, I'll introduce you to the various techniques and tools you will need to know in order to complete the projects in the book. Keep in mind that this is not a comprehensive list of all maneuvers that can be performed with Photoshop Elements. These techniques are specific to the projects contained within this book. I recommend reading through this section before you begin any of the projects. Experiment with the various tools and techniques so that you are familiar with them. Also use this section for reference as you go through the projects in the rest of the book.

BEFORE YOU BEGIN

I must emphasize that this book is not designed to be an operating manual for Photoshop Elements. Below is a list of basic computer functions that you should be able to perform and prerequisite materials you should have before attempting techniques and projects in this book.

You should be able to:
install and open the Photoshop Elements application; use a mouse or graphics tablet; open a file; use menus and toolbars; operate a digital camera; import photos to your computer and retrieve them; operate a scanner.

Materials you will need:
computer; Photoshop Elements, preferably version 6.0 or higher (trial versions are available online at www.adobe.com); digital camera; scanner; graphics tablet (optional, but preferred).

SETTING UP

Working file
In the projects, you will often be working with several files at once. However, there will be one primary file to which you'll add imagery and make alterations. I will refer to this main file as your "working file." Sometimes the files will be duplicates of photos, and sometimes they will be new blank files.

Creating a new blank file
When you want to create a new file with a transparent or solid-colored background go to **File>New>Blank File**.

Resolution
If you plan on printing your artwork, make sure the images you use are high resolution, meaning at least 300 dpi (72 dpi is intended for posting to the Web). This will allow you to print high-quality artwork. (If a digital photo you take is 72 dpi in a very large size [see Fig. 1], this is still high quality. But you should change the resolution of the image in Photoshop Elements to 300 dpi before working with it.) To ensure high-resolution photos, set your camera and scanner to a high quality.

To set up a file for printing purposes, go to **File>New**. Make your file at least 8" (20cm) wide and set its dpi resolution to 300. For the background, you can choose either white or transparent, depending on your needs.

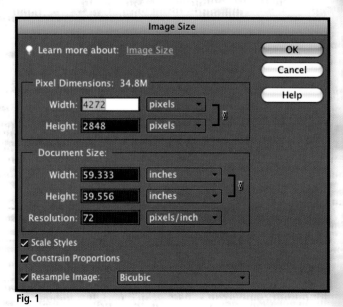

Fig. 1

■ Digital Detail

If you have a low-resolution image, you cannot make it a high-resolution image by merely increasing its dpi. Doing so will only result in a fuzzy photo, as there will not be enough pixels for clarity. To check the image size of your photo go to **Image>Resize>Image Size** *(see Fig. 1.) in the drop-down menu.*

Fig. 2

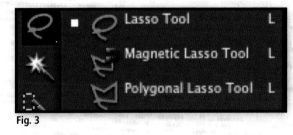

Fig. 3

When putting your artwork together, you will want the digital elements to be in proportion to one another. You can always decrease size without losing quality, but will lose quality if you increase the size. I have found, however, that you can use lower quality texture photos as layers for your artwork, as you will most likely be adjusting their blending modes and Opacity levels, masking the blurriness that results from the lower resolution.

Saving files

So that you can preserve the original, I recommend using copies of original images if they will be the working file (go to **File>Duplicate** to make a copy). When you want to save your working files, save them as a Photoshop (.psd) file in order to preserve all layers for future manipulation. When your work is complete and you do not need to save your layers for future manipulation, save the file as a JPEG (.jpg) or TIFF (.tif) file. If you plan on printing your artwork, make sure to save your image files at their highest quality. Also be sure to save files as you work.

SELECTING AND MOVING

Deselecting

You can easily deselect any selection by going to **Select>Deselect**.

Selecting and moving with the Move Tool

The Move Tool, located at the top of the Tools Palette (see Fig. 2), will be one of the most used. Click on the tool prior to selecting and moving layers as well as resizing and rotating. You can also use this tool to move one file of imagery to another.

Selecting areas with the Magic Wand Tool

The Magic Wand Tool lets you quickly select an area of consistent color (for example, a red dress) without having to trace its outline with one of the Lasso Tools. You can adjust the Tolerance of this tool. A low Tolerance level will select fewer colors that are similar to the pixel you clicked on. A higher Tolerance will select more pixels with a broader range of colors.

Selecting areas with the Lasso Tool

The Lasso Tool (see Fig. 3) allows you to make different types of selections. The basic Lasso Tool allows you to make a free-form selection. If you need more control when making your selection, I recommend using one of the other Lasso Tools.

The Magnetic Lasso Tool works well when selecting objects with fine details, especially if the object contrasts with the background. Trace around the object in its entirety, ending up exactly where you started (you'll see a small transparent circle) in order to select it. If you miss a part, just press the Shift key and trace around the area that you want to add to the existing selection. Using the Move Tool, you can then click and drag a selection.

Use the Polygonal Lasso Tool when selecting areas with straight lines and angles.

Selecting colors

To choose a paint color (to apply with tools such as the Brush Tool, Pencil Tool and Paint Bucket Tool), click on the Set Foreground Color box at the bottom of the Tools Palette (see Fig. 4). A box will open, allowing you to choose from a broad range of hues. To choose a background color, click on the box behind the foreground color box.

Fig. 4

WORKING WITH LAYERS

Layers in Photoshop Elements are like the layers of paint and paper you build up as you create a mixed-media collage, where some of the new layers completely cover what is below, while others allow lower layers to show through. In Photoshop Elements any new layer you add will cover the layers below. You can reveal the layers beneath by using the Eraser Tool, reducing the Opacity of layers or by applying blending modes.

Layers Palette

The Layers Palette (see Fig. 5) shows each new layer you create; essentially they are stacked one on top of the other. These layers can be manipulated in a variety of ways (as you will see). You can turn layers on and off while you work—just click on the "eye" icon to the left of a layer in the Layers Palette, experimenting until you find just the right look. You can delete a layer by selecting it in the Layers Palette and then clicking the trash can icon at the top of the Layers Palette.

Converting the Background layer

To protect the original image, the Background layer is locked. To alter the layer, you must unlock it by converting it to a regular layer. Double click on the Background layer in the Layers Palette and rename it Layer 0 (the default name).

Creating a new layer

Whenever you add an image to your piece (e.g., dragging a new photo into your working file) the program automatically puts it on its own new layer. You can also create a new layer manually by going to **Layer>New>Layer,** which is helpful when you are adding brushstrokes.

Duplicating a layer

Layer>Duplicate Layer
You can make a copy of any layer in your piece with this command. Select the layer you want to duplicate first by clicking on it in the working file or in the Layers Palette. The copy will appear directly over the layer you have copied. Use the Move Tool to click and drag it to your desired location.

■Digital Detail

Keep in mind that if a tool is not working as you expect it to, you may have a small selection you're not aware of. Choose the Deselect command and try the tool again.

Fig. 5

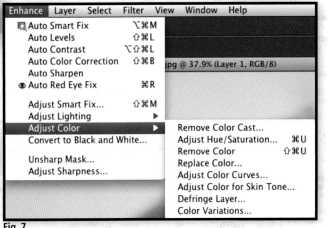
Fig. 6

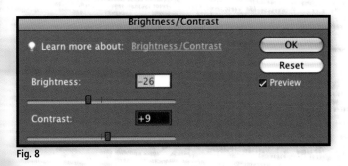
Fig. 7

Fig. 8

Arranging layers

There are two ways to arrange layers, which refers to moving a layer forward or backward in a file: (1) select the layer in the working file and go to **Layer>Arrange**; (2) click the layer in the Layers Palette and drag it up to move it forward and down to move it back.

Merging layers

To organize and simplfy working files, you can combine multiple layers, making them into one layer. (Just be sure you will not want to manipulate the layers later on.) To do this, select the layers you want to merge in your Layers Palette by holding down the Command key (the Ctrl key on a PC). At the same time, click on the layers you want to merge. They will be highlighted once you click on them. Release the Command key when you have finished selecting the layers. Then, go to **Layer>Merge Visible** (see Fig. 6) to merge them. Keep in mind that once layers are merged, they cannot be changed (only added to). Flattening an image (**Layer>Flatten Image**) merges all layers, and also turns transparent areas to white.

MAKING ADJUSTMENTS

You can find most of the menus for making adjustments under the Enhance Menu (see Fig. 7). I recommend using adjustment layers when possible (**Layer>New Adjustment Layer**), which are essentially duplicates of the base image. They allow you to make a variety of adjustments to your piece while keeping your original layer intact. This way, you can change or remove the adjustments later. You can also adjust the blending mode and Opacity of an adjustment layer.

Brightness/Contrast
Enhance>Adjust Lighting>Brightness/Contrast
Layer>New Adjustment Layer>Brightness/Contrast
This adjustment allows you to easily manipulate the tonal range of your imagery. If you move the brightness slider to the right, you will increase tonal values and highlights. If you move it to the left (see Fig. 8), you will decrease values and increase shadows. The contrast slider allows you to increase or decrease the range of tonal values in your imagery.

Color Curves
Enhance>Adjust Color>Adjust Color Curves
Use this command to adjust the tonal range of your imagery. You can adjust up to 14 different points of an image's tonal range, from shadows to highlights, giving you more control than you get when using the Brightness/Contrast Menu.

Color and shadows with Adjust Smart Fix

Enhance>Adjust Smart Fix

This automatic feature corrects the overall color balance and improves shadow and highlight detail.

Hue/Saturation

Enhance>Adjust Color>Adjust Hue/Saturation
Layer>New Adjustment Layer>Hue/Saturation

This command lets you manipulate the hue, saturation and lightness of either a specific color or all colors at once. You can manipulate individual colors by selecting them in the Edit drop-down menu. Check the Colorize box (see Fig. 9) to change an image to shades of just one color.

Opacity

You can adjust the Opacity levels of a layer by clicking on the layer in the Layers Palette and moving the Opacity slider (see Fig. 10) located at the top of the Layers Palette. You can also adjust the Opacity of various tools in their respective toolbars. Just move the slider to the left to increase transparency.

Shadows/Highlights

Enhance>Adjust Lighting>Shadows/Highlights

This feature allows you to darken or lighten shadows and high-lights, and increase or reduce the contrast of middle tones.

Sharpness

Enhance>Adjust Sharpness

You can increase the clarity of your imagery with this feature. Keep in mind that too much sharpness will give your image a grainy look.

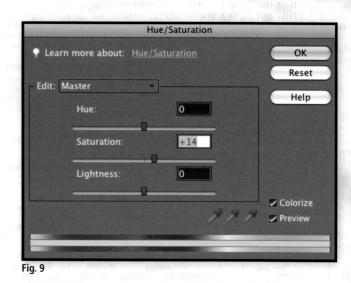
Fig. 9

Fig. 10

BLENDING MODES

Blending modes control the way layers interact with each other. In the simplest terms, they allow you to blend one layer with another. There are numerous blending modes available in Photoshop Elements, and each one produces a different effect. The blending modes and their basic descriptions are listed in this section. The best way to learn about these effects is to try them out on your projects. Start with a digital photo and add a texture photo to it. Apply a blending mode to this new layer, and see what happens!

You can adjust the blending mode of a layer by clicking on the layer in your working file or in the Layers Palette. Then make a selection from the blending mode drop-down menu located at the top of the Layers Palette (see Fig. 11).

Normal is often referred to as the default mode or threshold. Choosing this mode will not alter your imagery.

Dissolve results in a random replacement of the pixels, producing a dissolved effect.

Darken selects the base or blend color (whichever is darker) as the result color.

Multiply multiplies the base color by the blend color, so the result color is always darker.

Color Burn darkens the base color to reflect the blend color by increasing the contrast.

Linear Burn darkens the base color to reflect the blend color by decreasing the brightness.

Darker Color displays the lower value color.

Lighten selects the base or blend color (whichever is lighter).

Screen multiplies the inverse of the blend and base colors. The result color is always a lighter color.

Color Dodge brightens the base color to reflect the blend color by decreasing the contrast.

Linear Dodge brightens the base color to reflect the blend color by increasing the brightness.

Lighter Color displays the higher value color.

Overlay multiplies or screens the colors, depending on the base color. The highlights and shadows of the base color are preserved.

Soft Light darkens or lightens the colors, depending on the blend color.

Hard Light multiplies or screens the colors, depending on the blend color. The effect looks like a bright spotlight.

Vivid Light burns or dodges the colors by increasing or decreasing the contrast, depending on the blend color.

Linear Light burns or dodges the colors by decreasing or increasing the brightness, depending on the blend color.

Pin Light replaces the base color with the blend color, sometimes producing no change, depending on the tonal values.

Hard Mix adds the red, green and blue channel values of the blend color to the RGB values of the base color, therefore changing all pixels to primary colors—red, green, blue, cyan, yellow, magenta, white or black.

Difference subtracts either the blend color from the base color or the base color from the blend color, depending on which has the greater brightness value. Blending with white inverts the base color values, and blending with black produces no change.

Exclusion creates an effect that is similar to Difference, but lower in contrast.

Hue creates a result color with the brightness and saturation of the base color and the hue of the blend color.

Saturation creates a result color with the brightness and hue of the base color and the saturation of the blend color.

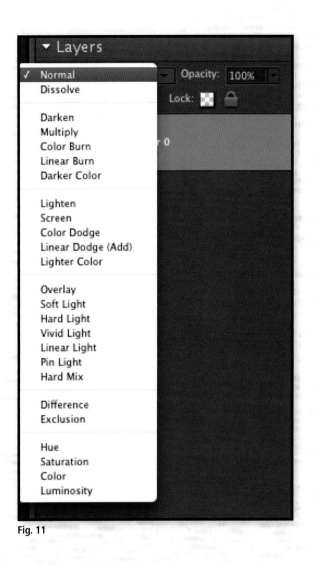

Fig. 11

Color creates a result color with the brightness of the base color and the hue and saturation of the blend.

Luminosity creates a result color with the hue and saturation of the base color and the brightness of the blend color. This mode creates the inverse effect of Color mode.

Note that you can adjust the Opacity of a layer that you applied a blending mode to. I often do this if the effect is too harsh with the Opacity set at 100% (the default).

APPLYING FILTERS AND EFFECTS

You can access filters in two locations—either by going to the Filter Menu at the top of your screen (see Fig. 12), or by going to the Effects Palette (see Fig. 13) located above the Layers Palette. The Effects Palette provides numerous possibilities for your imagery—the effects are categorized by Filters, Layer Styles and Photo Effects (see the icons at the top of the Effects Palette). In the Effects Palette you can see thumbnails that demonstrate the look of each effect. (Note: If you want to preview and adjust various filters on your actual imagery, go to **Filter>Filter Gallery**.) Below is a description of the filters you'll apply to the projects in the book, though there are many more filters to try.

Filters

Invert Filter: Filter>Adjustments>Invert or Layer>New Adjustment Layer>Invert. This command inverts the colors in your imagery. (Note: Color print film contains an orange mask in its base. Therefore, the invert command cannot make accurate positive images from their scanned color negatives.)

Lighting Effects: Filter>Render>Lighting Effects. If you want to add lighting effects to your piece, choose from the many Styles (e.g., Flashlight, Flood Light, Soft Spotlight) and Light Types (e.g., Directional, Omni, Spotlight). Further adjustments will allow you to manipulate Intensity, Focus and other properties.

Colored Pencil Filter: Filter>Artistic>Colored Pencil. This particular filter will make your imagery appear as if it were sketched with colored pencils. You can adjust Pencil Width, Stroke Pressure and Paper Brightness.

Dry Brush Filter: Filter>Artistic>Dry Brush. This filter makes imagery appear as if you painted it with a dry-brush effect. You can adjust Brush Size, Brush Detail and Texture.

Gaussian Blur Filter: Filter>Blur>Gaussian Blur. This effect will quickly blur a selection, allow you to adjust its intensity and add a hazy effect to your imagery.

Motion Blur Filter: Filter>Blur>Motion Blur. This will blur your imagery in a specified direction and intensity.

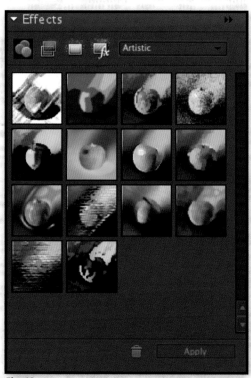

Fig. 12

Fig. 13

14

Texture Filter: Filter>Texture. This will apply an array of beautiful textures to your imagery (e.g., Craquelure, Grain, Mosaic Tiles).

Photo Filter: Filter>Adjustments>Photo Filter or Layer>New Adjustment Layer>Photo Filter. Use this to apply color filters to your imagery (e.g., warming and cooling filters). You can adjust the settings of each filter. If you apply the filter as a new adjustment layer, it appears as its own layer. You can then apply a blending mode and reduce the Opacity to produce more subtle changes.

Poster Edges Filter: Filter>Artistic>Poster Edges. With this filter, you can reduce the number of colors in your imagery and define edges with black lines.

Texturizer Filter: Filter>Texture>Texturizer. Choose Brick, Burlap, Canvas or Sandstone textures and play with various settings.

Fill layers

Solid Color Fill Layer: Layer>New Fill Layer>Solid Color (see Fig. 14)
You can apply a layer of solid color to your imagery with this effect. I often use it to tint a photo or elements of a photo. You can apply a blending mode to this type of layer to produce further interesting effects, and reduce its Opacity level to produce more subtle colorizing effects.

Gradient Fill Layer: Layer>New Fill Layer>Gradient
A gradient is a smooth blending of shades from light to dark. Gradient Fill Layers produce this kind of effect. You can apply a blending mode or change the Opacity of a Gradient Fill Layer. This can be done either in the Gradient Fill Layer Menu (see Fig. 15) or in the Layers Palette. I enjoy applying blending modes that have lighting effects (e.g., Hard Light, Soft Light, Vivid Light), as seen in *Between Worlds* on page 110.

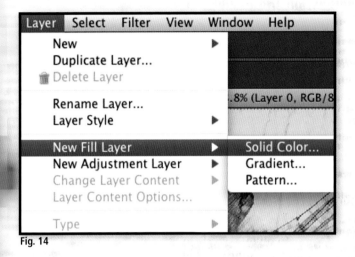

Fig. 14

Fig. 15

MISCELLANEOUS TECHNIQUES

Duplicating a file

Going to **File>Duplicate** will make an exact copy of a file you have opened. If you are starting with a photo that will be your working file, it is a good idea to make a duplicate of it first.

Duplicating a selection

To duplicate a selection, you first need to select it with one of the Lasso Tools. Then go to **Edit>Copy** and then **Edit>Paste**. The duplicate will appear directly over the selection you have copied. Use the Move Tool to click and drag it to your desired location.

Feathering edges of a selection

To soften or blur the edges of a selection you have made with one of the Lasso Tools, go to **Select>Feather**. You can set the Feather Radius as desired—the higher the number, the greater the feathering effect. Some of the details on the edge of the selection will be lost. You really notice the effect of this tool when you move the selection to your desired spot.

Loading a custom brush

If you download a custom brush you will need to load it into the Brushes Menu, which is located in the upper left-hand corner of the Brush Toolbar. To load a brush or brushes from a folder on the hard drive to a designated brush palette in the Brushes Menu, you'll need to click on the double arrow on the right-hand side of the brush palette and select Load Brushes (see Fig. 16). Follow the steps to retrieving your brushes from their folder on the hard drive. Your set will appear in the Brushes Menu. Keep in mind that if you switch to another brush set, your newly-loaded set will probably disappear. If you wish to use that set again, you will have to reload it from your hard drive. (Refer to page 93 in Chapter 4 for details on creating your own custom brushes.)

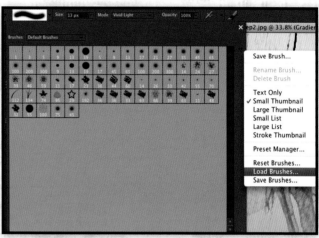

Fig. 16

Resizing

To resize a layer, select the Move Tool, then click on the layer (in your working file) and drag on the hollow squares located at the edges and corners of the image. Press the Shift key while resizing your object to maintain its proportions.

Rotating and flipping

The rotating and flipping options are located at **Image>Rotate** (see Fig. 17). The first six choices allow you to rotate or flip the entire working file. The next six allow you to rotate or flip a layer.

Rotating freely

You can free-rotate a layer in two similar ways: (1) select the layer then click on the hollow circle at the bottom, center of the layer (see Fig. 18) and drag to rotate; (2) select the layer, place your cursor on top of one of the hollow squares until it becomes an arched arrow, and then drag to rotate. Make sure the Move Tool is selected before rotating. To rotate a layer a specific amount of degrees and in a specific direction, go to **Image>Rotate**.

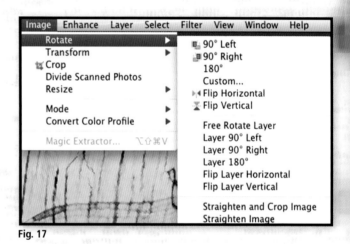

Fig. 17

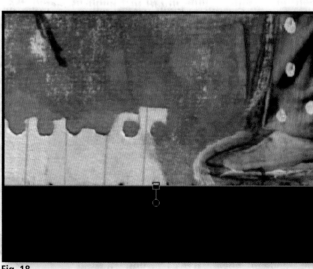

Fig. 18

Fig. 19

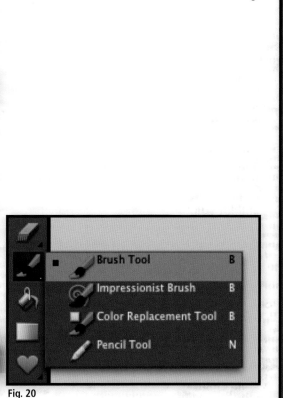

Fig. 20

USING TOOLS

We've already discussed some of the tools (Move, Lasso, Pencil). Below are explanations of other tools in the Tools Palette (see Fig. 19) that you will be using in the projects. Note that each tool has its own toolbar, with further options, located at the top of the screen when the tool is selected.

Blur Tool

This tool softens hard edges and blurs details. The more you go over an area with this tool, the blurrier it becomes.

Brush/Pencil Tool

Both the Brush Tool and the Pencil Tool (see Fig. 20) allow you to draw. The Brush Tool creates softer strokes, while the Pencil Tool creates hard-edged lines. You can chose your Brush type and adjust Size, Mode (blending mode) and Opacity in the Brush Toolbar. You can also explore additional options in the Additional Brush Options box (just click on the paintbrush icon to the right of the Opacity setting). You can chose various brush presets when using a variety of tools besides the Brush and Pencil tools.

Burn/Dodge Tool

Both the Burn Tool and the Dodge Tool are based on traditional photography techniques that regulate exposure on select areas of a print. The Burn Tool will darken areas of your image, while the Dodge Tool will lighten them.

Clone Stamp Tool

This tool allows you to copy areas of an image to other areas. To use the tool, press Option (Alt on a PC) while clicking the cursor over the area you want to copy, and then release the key. Then click the cursor (keeping the mouse depressed) over the area you want to change. When you are cloning, a cross will appear, showing you what area you are copying. You can adjust the settings in the toolbar.

Color Replacement Tool

Located in the Brush Tool fly-out menu, you can replace specific colors in your piece with this tool. (For example, you can paint over all red areas with yellow.) You can adjust the settings in the toolbar. You'll have to adjust the Tolerance level depending on the colors in your photo (a low tolerance will replace colors very similar to the pixels you click, and a higher number will replace a broader range of colors). Choose a foreground color to be the new color by clicking on the Set Foreground Color box. Then click on the Set Background Color box to select the color you want to replace. (Use the eyedropper to pull color from the working file.)

Crop Tool

Cut out unwanted portions of your imagery with this tool. Select the portion of the image that you want to keep and click on the green check mark at the bottom right corner of the selection to perform the crop. In the toolbar, you can choose a standard ratio size or specify a custom size for your crop.

Eraser Tool

I use this tool to clean up the edges of selections and other undesirable areas. For best results, zoom in on an area (using the Zoom Tool). If you select a background color and use the eraser, it will apply the background color you selected. If you have not selected a background color, it will make the pixels you erase white (or transparent, if your file is transparent).

Eyedropper Tool

This tool will pick up color from an area of your working file (or any other open file) and designate it as the foreground color; just click on the desired color.

Marquee Tool

Use this tool to make an elliptical or rectangular selection. If you want to make a circular or square selection, press the Shift key when selecting.

Paint Bucket Tool

This tool fills in areas with a color with one click. If you choose a foreground color and click on your piece, the Paint Bucket Tool will fill the pixels you clicked with the color, as well as fill all similar pixels (e.g., if you have a simple circle, it will fill the entire circle; if you have a detailed photo, it will fill smaller areas). Experiment with Tolerance (the higher this level, the more paint will be applied in one click). Further options include Anti-alias (to smooth edges), Contiguous (to fill pixels that are contiguous to the one you clicked on) and All Layers (to fill pixels on all visible layers). If you wish to apply a pattern rather than a solid color, choose a pattern from the Paint Bucket Toolbar.

Type Tool

If you choose this tool and click in your working file, a blinking line will appear. You can begin typing just as you would in a document, entering and editing the type in much the same way. In the toolbar, you can choose a font and color, adjust its size and style and select alignment. You can create warped text (the T over the arch—see Fig. 21) and change text orientation (to the right of the warped text icon). The best way to discover possibilities is to play!

Zoom Tool

This tool is a favorite of mine when it comes to doing detail work in conjunction with other tools. The Zoom Tool is located at the top of the Tools Palette. In the toolbar, chose "+" and click on your project to zoom in close. Choose "–" to pull back to actual size or smaller. You can also press the Option (Alt on a PC) key to change the zoom direction.

■Digital Detail

You can make a selection with either a Lasso Tool or Marquee Tool and fill the selection with paint from the Paint Bucket Tool.

■Digital Detail

To give a smooth edge to the areas you select, click the Anti-alias box in the toolbar at the top of the screen.

Fig. 21

■Digital Detail

When working with the Brush Tool, Pencil Tool or Paint Bucket Tool, pressing Option (Alt on a PC) lets you select a color from an image, turning it into paint color.

WHAT YOU'LL NEED

The What You'll Need section at the beginning of each project tells you what digital materials you will need to complete the project, as well as what techniques you will need to know how to perform. Keep in mind the following information as you go through the projects.

TECHNICAL SKILLS

The instructions for each project are intended to show you how to build various types of digital art. Many of the tools and techniques are similar among the projects. As such, the instructions do not include information about the essential techniques and tools described earlier. The skills list outlines the essential techniques you will need to know how to perform in order to complete a project and the tools you will need to know how to use. The page numbers refer back to the instructions on pages 8–18.

The photos below show the types of images you will be working with in the projects. From top to bottom, they are: a subject photo, a texture photo and an environment photo. You can find these three photos on the book CD.

DIGITAL MATERIALS

This section outlines all the necessary digital files you will need to complete the project. I recommend gathering all your materials prior to starting the project. You're welcome to any of the same images that I used in my own projects; I've included the sources for all the materials I used in my projects (that aren't my own creation). And don't forget about the CD included with the book!

Background photo: You'll want to chose imagery that would be suitable for a background. Natural elements like grass, trees, flowers and clouds make for great backgrounds, as do repeating prints and patterns.

Environment photo: This refers to a photo of a background in which you could place a subject, such as a room indoors or an outdoor landscape, like a field or forest.

Subject photo: This will be the focus of your digital art and usually what will be placed on top of the environment photo. The subject does not need to be a person (an animal might work for the project).

Texture photo: You'll want to choose imagery of textures. I typically specify what type of texture you need, such as a rough texture (like rust or concerete), natural (like wood) or vintage (like old parchment).

Additional photo: This refers to other imagery you will need. If I don't specify a type, you can choose whatever you like!

Font: You can use fonts installed on your system or download free ones.

Custom brush: This is a brush that is not already installed in the program. You can find them online or make your own (see page 93). In most cases, when a project calls for a custom brush, you can substitute one of the preinstalled brushes to create a similar look.

1

Manipulating Images

Digital photomanipulation is exactly what it sounds like. It is digital manipulation of imagery through the use of image-editing software. In this chapter, you will digitally manipulate either a single photo or a combination of two photos.

I will teach you how to apply effects that will take your photographs to a whole new level. Learn to make just part of a photo pop with color. Create a vignette effect by darkening the edges of your imagery. Add textural layers to your imagery for added interest and intrigue. You will find that these techniques not only enhance your photos and change their physical appearance, but they also bring a sort of poetry to them, adding new artistic dimension and depth.

WHISPERS
Creating Vignettes With Color Fill Layers

I turned a corner in one of my favorite local antique stores, and there she was—this vintage doll with such allure. She had stories to tell, whispering of her past and the little girl who cared for her so many years ago. To create a feeling of intrigue, as of an unknown past, I added a vignette effect to the photo. Creating a vignette by darkening the edges of your photo will give your image an eerie, mysterious quality. In other words, I wouldn't recommend this type of vignette effect for wedding photos—unless, of course, you are going for a Gothic look.

DIGITAL MATERIALS

Subject photo

Sources for Project Artwork

○ Photo of doll: book CD

TECHNICAL SKILLS

Duplicating a file (p. 15)

Feathering (p. 16)

Adding a Solid Color Fill Layer (p. 15)

Adjusting the Opacity of a layer (p. 12)

Merging layers/flattening an image (p. 11)

Using Tools:

Marquee Tool (p. 18)

Eraser Tool (p. 18)

Duplicate the file
Open the photo and duplicate it. This will be your working file.

Select focal point of photo
Select the focal point of the photo with the Elliptical Marquee Tool. (Press Shift to select a perfect circle.) Here, I selected the doll's head and shoulders.

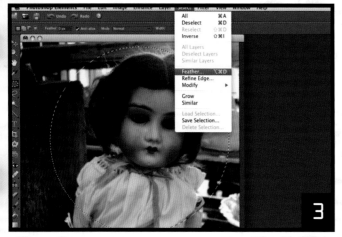

Feather edges of selection

Feather the edges of the selection. Set the Feather Radius to 40 pixels.

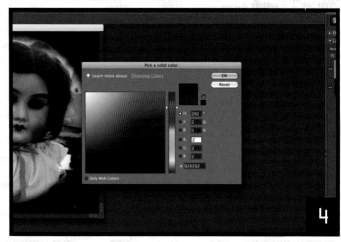

Add fill layer of solid color

Now darken the outside of the circular selection. Go to SELECT>INVERSE to select the area. Add a New Fill Layer with solid color. Choose black with the eyedropper and click OK.

Blend vignette's edges with background

Reduce the Opacity of the layer to about 70%. Then use the Eraser Tool, set to 29% Opacity to erase parts of the oval's edges. This will blend the vignette's edges with the background. When you're finished, flatten the image and save the file.

■Digital Detail

Determine what kind of a look you want when creating a vignette: Do you want there to be just a hint of vignette, or do you want something bolder and well-defined? I tend to think "subtle" when creating a vignette layer—I usually don't want the edges to be too dark and tend to prefer a soft-looking circle. I take advantage of both the Feathering option and Eraser Tool set to a low Opacity to create this soft type of vignette. For a wonderful example of a more well-defined vignette style, see contributing artist Sonya Cullimore's piece on the next page.

KAWAU | BY SONYA CULLIMORE

The silhouette of the bird and the tree branches against the sky caught Sonya's eye. Zooming her camera lens in allowed her to emphasize and crop the subject more tightly. Sonya executed a vignette with this photo in a similar manner to the main project using Corel Paint Shop Pro. The contrast of the dark area and silhouetted images with the light sky give a wonderful eerie quality.

CREDITS
Software: Corel Paint Shop Pro

Technique to Try
Create a vignette using a high-contrast photo. Leave the fill layer black without reducing its Opacity.

THE JACKS
Popping Areas of Color

Each Halloween in the small Maine town I live in, residents look forward to seeing a fabulous display of jack-o'-lanterns put together by a local family, artfully arranged on the old stone wall of their farmstead, which is pictured here. Adding a pop of color was the perfect effect for this photo—it makes the jacks shine. When you want the importance of an element (or elements) in your photo to be emphasized, one artistic approach is to maintain the color of this element and desaturate the rest of the photo. The sentimental meaning inherent in the object will become enhanced, and you will find that the element with color will really pop out. Boo!

WHAT YOU'LL NEED

DIGITAL MATERIALS
Subject photo

TECHNICAL SKILLS

Duplicating a file (p. 15)

Converting Background to Layer 0 (p. 10)

Adjusting Hue/Saturation (p. 12)

Deselecting an object (p. 10)

Adjusting Brightness/Contrast (p. 11)

Arranging layers (p. 11)

Adjusting the Opacity of a layer (p. 12)

Merging layers (p. 11)

Duplicating a layer (p. 10)

Apply the Gaussian Blur Filter (p. 14)

Using Tools:

Lasso Tool (p. 9)

Clone Stamp Tool (p. 17)

Select area(s) to remain in color

Create a duplicate of your photo. This will be your working file. Convert the Background layer to Layer 0. Using the Magnetic Lasso Tool, select one area of the photo you want to remain in color. Then press Shift and select another area. Repeat until all areas are selected. Here, I selected the jack-o'-lanterns.

Remove color in background

Since you will want to maintain the color of the selected area and lose the color in the rest of the photo, go to SELECT>INVERSE. Now the fun part! Open the Hue/Saturation Menu. Keep the Edit setting set to Master. Move the Saturation slider all the way to the left (–100), making the selected area black and white. Then deselect everything in the working file.

Adjust edges as needed

Now you can adjust as needed. (Here, I noticed some of the pumpkins' edges were changed to gray, and there were other areas where the background was still in color.) Zoom in very close on the edges of the colored areas. Select the Clone Stamp Tool and set the brush size small. To paint gray areas in color, clone some of the color and copy that into any unwanted gray areas. Use the same technique to make any unwanted colored areas gray.

Increase contrast

Colors (and gray areas) can get a bit dull, so punch up your contrast as desired using the Brightness/Contrast Menu. For my piece, I left Brightness at 0 and set Contrast to +36. Now that makes the color pop!

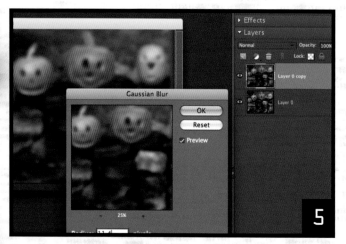

Duplicate layer and apply Gaussian Blur Filter

To give my piece an eerie effect, perfect for Halloween, I performed one of my favorite tricks! Giving a diffused light effect works well for a variety of projects. To apply the look, first make sure you only have one layer (Layer 0). (If needed, merge all the layers.) Duplicate that layer then apply a Gaussian Blur Filter to the duplicate layer. Set the Radius to 11.4 pixels.

Reduce Opacity of Layer 0

Arrange the layers so that Layer 0 Copy is behind Layer 0 (select Send to Back). In the Layers Palette, select Layer 0. Set the Opacity to 60%. When the piece is complete, flatten the image and save the file.

READ THE SIGNS | BY SONYA CULLIMORE

Sonya discovered this clever stop sign graffiti while waiting at an intersection. After finding a place to park the car, she went back to take the photo. To make the sign stand out, Sonya used the same color-pop effect but with a slightly different approach. She duplicated the photo (by duplicating the background layer) and desaturated the color of the entire layer. Then she selected the stop sign on the duplicated layer using the Freehand Selection Tool, and deleted the selection, revealing the colored stop sign on the Background layer beneath.

CREDITS
Software: Corel Paint Shop Pro

Technique to Try
Create another piece with pops of color, but this time try Sonya Cullimore's method described above.

UNBOUND
Designing With Type

■ Digital Detail

*The Web abounds with sources for fun
(and free!) fonts to use, including:
www.1001freefonts.com
www.dafont.com
www.urbanfonts.com
www.fonts.com*

Are you being you? At every turn, we are bombarded with messages telling us how to be. Sometimes they get so loud, we forget to listen to our inner voice. Blaring are the advertisements on what types of things we must have. The media controls what information we are exposed to and often dictates how we should think. This piece is a reflection on these observations, which I think about often and try to be mindful of. It's about clearing away the noise, resisting conformity and deciding for ourselves who we really are and who we really want to be. It's time to color outside the lines.

This particular project will show you fun ways to incorporate text in your piece. You'll learn how to combine a variety of fonts and text colors to create interest, rotate and warp text, and adjust text layer Opacity levels.

Duplicate a mannequin photo
Open the two photos of mannequins. Make a duplicate of one photo. This will be your working file.

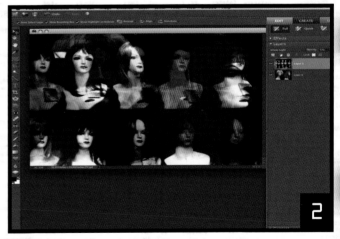

Add other photo and adjust layer
Change the Background layer of the working file to Layer 0. Then move the other mannequin photo (which will become Layer 1) into the working file. Set the blending mode of Layer 1 to Linear Light and adjust the Opacity to 77%. Merge the two layers.

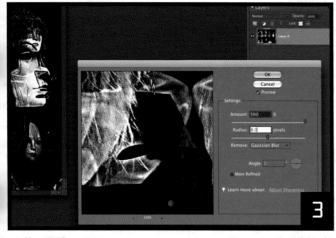

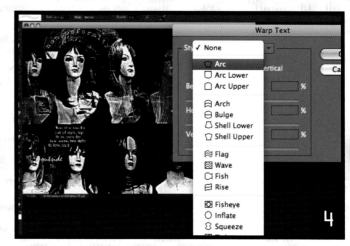

Adjust sharpness

Open the Sharpness Menu and adjust the sharpness of your new Layer 0. Set the levels as follows: Amount: 500%; Radius: 8.0 pixels; Remove: Gaussian Blur; Angle: 0. Adjusting the sharpness to an extreme level makes the smooth, realistic quality of the mannequins transform into imagery that looks more like a painting or drawing.

Add text layers

Select the Type Tool. Type various phrases into different layers in the working file. Choose different fonts, sizes and colors for different phrases, and play with the warped text icon. Font, size, color selection and warped text controls appear in the Type Toolbar. Then change the Opacity of some of the text layers, as desired.

Add main text and apply custom brush

Select a color and font. Type your main text across the image (here, I typed "it is up to you"). Then load a custom grunge brush (or just select a grunge-like brush in the Brushes Palette). In white at a low Opacity, stamp the brush all over the piece.

    Next, if you have a graphics tablet and pen, outline the text using the Pencil Tool. I used the Hard Mechanical 4 pixels brush located in the Basic Brushes palette. Alternatively, you can simply add a stroke to the letters. First go to LAYER>SIMPLIFY LAYER. Then EDIT>STROKE (OUTLINE) SELECTION. Choose a width of 1 pixel and adjust the other settings as desired. When the piece is complete, flatten the image and save the file.

■Digital Detail

Here are some tips for working creatively with text:

- *When you are experimenting with warped text, you may also want to try more styles in the Style drop-down menu in the Type Toolbar.*
- *Try rotating some text layers for added interest.*
- *You can add effects to your text using the various options in the Effects Palette.*

UNTITLED | BY CHRIS BROWN

"With all my designs, it's about striking a perfect balance between the photo and the graphic elements," says Chris. He designed this unpublished layout for his magazine Refueled. Instead of using the Text Tool to achieve warped text, Chris used sets of custom brushes designed with text.

CREDITS
Photo: Cheryl Schulke
Software: Adobe Photoshop CS2 and Adobe Illustrator CS2

Technique to Try

Instead of using the Type Tool to achieve rotated and warped text, download and install a variety of custom brush alphabets. (Check out the selection of custom alphabet brushes at www.graphicxtras.com.) To find out how to load brushes, see page 16.

ST. AUGUSTINE
Overlaying Texture

Grungy marks, scratches and stains can add character to a photo, as they do in this photo that I took of a pier on a beach in St. Augustine while on a family vacation. These effects can be easily achieved with the use of a texture overlay, which essentially is just a textural image imposed over your photo with a reduced Opacity level. You can apply a blending mode to the texture layer for interesting outcomes. I like to take photos to create a stash of my own textures. Textures that yield funky results include rusty metal, concrete floors, peeling and chipping paint, scratched surfaces, windows covered in raindrops and frosty fields. Have fun building up your own stock of images!

WHAT YOU'LL NEED

DIGITAL MATERIALS

Environment photo: of water (such as the ocean, a pier, a lake shore, a river, etc.)

Texture photo: grunge texture

Sources for Project Artwork

- Photo of pier: book CD
- Texture: book CD

TECHNICAL SKILLS

Duplicating a file (p. 15)

Converting Background to Layer 0 (p. 10)

Moving a file into another (p. 9)

Resizing (p. 16)

Adjusting the blending mode of a layer (p. 12)

Adjusting the Opacity of a layer (p. 12)

Merging layers/flattening an image (p. 11)

Adjusting Hue/Saturation (p. 12)

Using Tools:

Crop Tool (p. 17)

Duplicate photo of water
Create a duplicate of the photo of water. This will be your working file.

Add texture photo
Open the texture photo and move it into your working file, over the water photo (Background layer). Resize the texture photo (now Layer 1) as needed to fit the size of the working file.

Adjust mode and Opacity of texture layer

Set the blending mode of Layer 1 (the texture photo) to Color Burn and the Opacity to 59%.

Crop image

Crop the photo (as needed) to a roughly square size. If you'd like to choose a specific crop ratio, use the Aspect Ratio drop-down menu in the Crop Toobar. You can click on either the Background layer or Layer 1 to crop.

Merge layers and adjust Hue/Saturation

Merge the Background and Layer 1. To give the photo a sea-green hue and a vintage feel, adjust the Hue/Saturation. I set Hue to –18 and Saturation to –42. When the piece is complete, save the file.

■ Digital Detail

WHISPERS OF TIME | BY CHRYSTI HYDECK

Eternal stillness haunts this piece and serves as a reminder that just one single, solitary moment is often all that is needed to distinguish light from darkness, flight from fear and how those seemingly divided conflicts are intertwined within us. This powerful photo of a split tree is combined with layers of handwritten papers, scratched-up windows, birds in flight and a speckled texture to create a timeless portrait that speaks to the whispers of time. Chrysti played with each layer's contrast and overlaying effects to achieve the dark mood the piece conveys.

CREDITS
Textures: Chrysti Hydeck (www.createwithchrysti.com) and Nichole Van (www.nicholev.com)
Software: Corel Paint Shop Pro Photo X2

Technique to Try
Convert your photos and texture layers to grayscale (black and white) before blending them. One easy way to do this is to go to ENHANCE>ADJUST COLOR>REMOVE COLOR.

2

Painting & Drawing

Do you have a fear of painting or drawing in a realistic style? I do. Given a blank canvas and too many of my own censoring thoughts, I am often left not knowing where to begin. Photoshop Elements can help you get over this fear. The program contains digital tools that will take you by the hand and make the process of painting and drawing in the traditional sense much easier. The Brush Tool presets contain every type of brush style imaginable, which you can further tweak to fit your needs. If you put your brushwork on individual layers, you can later tweak them even more, or even delete them if you are not satisfied, which really takes the pressure off and makes for a great learning tool. Photoshop Elements also has built-in filters—resembling watercolor, chalk and charcoal drawings, colored pencil and more—that allow you to transform your photos into sketches and paintings with the click of a button. So what are you waiting for? Hours of enjoyment await!

SWEET SLUMBER

Making Drawings with Artistic Filters: Colored Pencil

All parents have a collection of favorite photos of their children—this is a favorite that I have of my daughter. Naturally, I was drawn to create a rendering of it in Photoshop Elements, which I did with some filter action. Sometimes we all need a little immediate gratification, especially when it comes to our art-making. Photoshop Elements to the rescue! You will have endless fun altering your photographs with different Artistic Filters like Colored Pencil (which I used in this piece), Watercolor, Fresco, Dry Brush and more.

WHAT YOU'LL NEED

TECHNICAL SKILLS

Duplicating a file (p. 15)

Appling the Colored Pencil Filter (p. 14)

DIGITAL MATERIALS

Subject photo

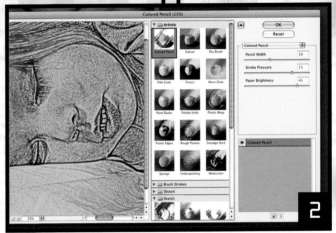

Duplicate photo

Open your photo and duplicate the file; this will be your working file. (Note that some photos yield better results than others. I prefer using photos that have light-colored backgrounds devoid of heavy detail. Darker colors and heavily detailed backgrounds can look too dark, heavy and muddy when you apply the Colored Pencil Filter.)

Apply Colored Pencil Filter

To turn the photo into a drawing, apply the Colored Pencil Filter. Play with the levels until you are satisfied with the results. I used the following settings: Pencil Width: 10; Stroke Pressure: 11; Paper Brightness: 41. Save the file.

INSPIRATION

FAIRY GHOST | BY SHONA COLE

Shona says, "After a photo shoot, I sometimes find a gem of a composition that begs me to take it a step further, like this one of my daughter. Creating the ghost figure came naturally once I saw the self-possessed pose and otherworldliness my camera caught." Shona set the foreground color of her photo to brown and the background color to pink, and then imposed a Chalk and Charcoal Filter. After applying the filter, she lightened the figure with the Brush Tool set to Color Dodge with a 30% Opacity. She also darkened the edges and background with the Brush Tool set to Color Burn with a 30% Opacity.

CREDITS
Software: Photoshop Elements 4.0

Technique to Try

Apply an artistic filter to a photo. Then apply one of the techniques you learned in Chapter 1 to enhance the new image.

SHINE LIGHT

Making Drawings with Artistic Filters: Colored Pencil + Dry Brush

This particular photo captured a magical, happenstance moment: My daughter noticed a dragonfly sitting on our deck railing one late fall afternoon. She sat there staring at it, studying its patterns and colors, until it flew away, to spend its last days before winter's dawn. I wanted to do the photo justice, so I altered it in Photoshop Elements, elevating it to the level of "real" art.

I am constantly amazed by the filter features available from Photoshop Elements that allow you to turn treasured photos into renderings of sketches and paintings. As you saw in the previous project, applying the Colored Pencil Filter (or other Artistic Filters) is a one-step wonder to instant digital art. Some photos, though, need a little extra attention to get the look you want. There's no rule against applying more than one filter in a project to give it some extra oomph. Here, the Dry Brush Filter gives just the lift this dragonfly needs.

WHAT YOU'LL NEED

TECHNICAL SKILLS

Duplicating a file (p. 15)

Applying the Colored Pencil Filter (p. 14)

Applying the Dry Brush Filter (p. 14)

DIGITAL MATERIALS

Subject photo

Apply Colored Pencil Filter

Open your photo and duplicate the file; this will be your working file. To turn the photo into a drawing, apply the Colored Pencil Filter. Play with the levels until you are satisfied with the results. I used the following settings: Pencil Width: 2; Stroke Pressure: 11; Paper Brightness: 44.

Apply Dry Brush Filter

To add definition and brilliance go back to the Filter Gallery and choose the Dry Brush Filter. I used the following settings: Brush Size: 8; Brush Detail: 10; Texture: 1. (Ah, much better!) Save the file.

INSPIRATION

COLORADO SUNRISE |

BY SHERI GAYNOR

This piece depicts Sheri's love for her life in the mountains and the inspiration the landscape has on her soul. To start the piece, she manipulated a digital photo using multiple filters, including Watercolor, Rough Pastels and Noise. She enhanced and changed colors using the Hue/Saturation Menu. Sheri added a layer of scanned antique wallpaper and reduced its Opacity level for a transparent effect. The burned image edges were created using Auto FX Software.

CREDITS
Software: Adobe Photoshop CS2; Auto FX Software (www.autofx.com)

Technique to Try

Turn a photo into a painting using at least two Artistic Filters. Then add a new layer (such as a texture) over the photo.

HARVEST
Replicating the Look of Traditional Painting

Give me acrylic paint, a variety of brushes, a water spritzer, canvas and paper towels and I will lose myself in abstract intuitive painting—it's one of my favorite modes of painting. During that time, I can easily go hand in hand with my muse into that joyful zone, where hours pass like the blink of an eye. In my art studio, I often enjoy creating large-scale paintings. I splat, scrape, add and pull off paint to create interesting effects using multiple layers of different media. Give me similar Photoshop Elements tools and I will do the same thing. For this particular project, I created an abstract intuitive painting using my digital tools.

Open new blank document

Set the background color to black. Then open a new blank file. Size it as desired (mine is 5" × 5" [13cm × 13cm]) with a resolution of 300. Set the Color Mode to RGB Color and set Background Contents to Background Color. This will be your working file. Change the Background layer to Layer 0.

Stamp first custom brush

Load your first custom brush and select it. I loaded a custom brush made to look like peeling paint. Size the brush very large (so it will be near the size of the working file) and select a new foreground color (I chose red) for the brush. Create a new layer and stamp the brush once on the new layer. Resize the layer as needed to fit the working file.

Digital Detail

If you don't have large custom brushes to load for this piece, you can create a similar look using the brushes that are already installed in the Brushes Menu in the Brush Toolbar. Instead of stamping once with a large brush, stamp multiple times to create the look of paint splotches and splatters.

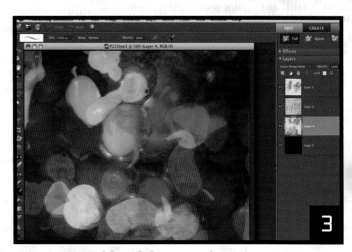

Stamp second brush in two colors

Load your second custom brush and select it. I loaded a custom brush made to look like paint splats. Size the brush very large and select a foreground color (I chose green) for the brush. Create a new layer and stamp the brush once on the new layer. Repeat to add additional colors on new layers. Then set the blending mode of the stamped layers to Linear Dodge, which increases the brightness and will result in some new, surprising colors.

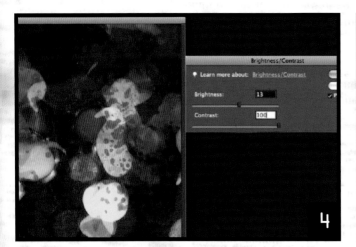

Rotate canvas and adjust lighting

When creating an abstract image like this, it's a good idea to rotate the canvas to vary the look of the stamp work. Then merge the visible layers. Adjust the Brightness/Contrast as desired. I changed the Brightness to +13 and Contrast to +100.

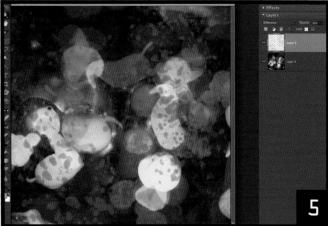

Add additional brushwork

If your piece needs more color or depth, just add some more brushwork! Choose one (or more) brushes and put each set of brushwork on a new layer. Adjust the blending mode and Opacity as needed. The colors in my piece weren't sitting right with me, so I added splashes of green with the Flat Bristle 111 pixels brush from the Thick Heavy Brushes drop-down menu. I then set the Opacity of the new layer to 36% and the blending mode to Difference, which made the green more orange (a nice surprise). I also added purple with the Soft Round 100 pixels brush from the Faux Finish Brushes drop-down menu. I set the blending mode to Hard Light and the Opacity to 76%.

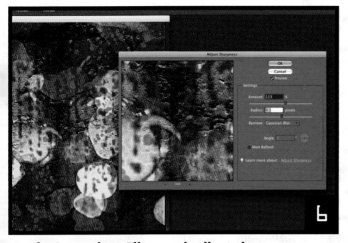

Apply Craquelure Filter and adjust sharpness

Merge the visible layers. To add texture and realism to the piece, apply
a filter. The Craquelure Filter (FILTER>TEXTURE>CRAQUELURE) will make your
work appear like you built the paint up in an impasto fashion. I set the
levels as follows: Crack Spacing: 77; Crack Depth: 6; Crack Brightness:
10. If the look of the piece is a bit fuzzy, adjust the sharpness.

Place in new file and add drop shadow

Open a blank file about 1" (3cm) larger than the working file. Set the
Resolution to 300, Color Mode to RGB Color and Background Content
to white. Then move the layer in the working file into the blank file. This
will be your new working file. Then go to the Effects Palette and click on
the Layer Styles icon. Choose Drop Shadows as the style and choose the
icon for Low. Double-click to apply the shadow. Click on the "fx" icon in
the Layers Palette to adjust the shadow's settings. Merge the layers.

Soften and adjust piece

To soften the piece, select white as the foreground color. Select the
Brush Tool and choose the Soft Round 100 pixels brush from the Faux
Finish Brushes drop-down menu and set it to an Opacity of 47%. Apply
the white, semi-transparent paint to random areas of your piece. If
you're not quite satisfied with the colors at this point, play with various
settings until you are. I felt my colors looked a little too bright, perhaps
a bit pseudo-neon. To correct this I went to the Adjust Smart Fix Menu
and set the Fix Amount to 100%. This step softened the colors a bit and
turned the electric pinks into purple hues.

■Digital Detail

*Adding a drop shadow is a great way to
make a digital piece look like an actual
three-dimensional painting. But this look
is most appropriate when using the image
alone—for example, for posting the image
online (as in a gallery) or simply printing
it on a sheet of paper. If you want to print
the piece and frame it like a traditional
piece of art, skip the drop shadow.*

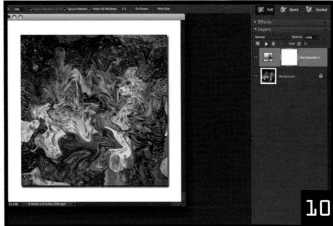

Apply Liquify Filter

Now you get to play around with one of the coolest tools—the Liquify Filter. Apply it by going to FILTER>DISTORT>LIQUIFY. Have fun pushing the pigment around, making swirly, blended, lava-lamp-like effects! I set the levels as follows: Brush Size: 211; Brush Pressure: 50.

Change Hue/Saturation

Adjust the colors once more using the Hue/Saturation Menu on a new adjustment layer. Following my muse, I played with both individual colors and the master setting. (I was feeling yellow.) When you're finished, save the file.

▊Digital Detail

There are numerous Web sites where you can download all sorts of custom brushes. You'll find everything from splotches and stains to florals and flames. Here are just a few site to check out:

www.photoshopbrushes.com
www.deviantart.com
www.obsidiandawn.com
www.angelic-trust.net/brushes/allbrushes.php
www.inobscuro.com

TEMPERANCE |

BY KELLY SHERIDAN

Temperance, a digitally-illustrated tarot card, is a beautiful example of replicating traditional painting in the realistic style in which artist Kelly Sheridan has been rigorously educated. Kelly created this digital painting by drawing freehand using a graphics tablet. Kelly added color using standard Photoshop brushes. For skin, she typically uses soft, diffuse brushes at a reduced Opacity and builds up layers in order to achieve luminosity. In all, the painting is made up of around fifty layers.

CREDITS
Software: Adobe Photoshop 7; Corel Painter 8; Alias Sketchbook Pro (Autodesk); Wacom graphics tablet

Technique to Try
Replicate traditional painting in a piece, but this time start with a drawing rather than abstract elements. If you're not comfortable drawing freehand digitally, scan an actual drawing and start there.

XIV
TEMPERANCE

VERUCA'S DREAM

Painting with Color Fill Layers

My friend Lori Vrba is one of the most gifted photographers I know. She has this remarkable, uncanny ability to capture the souls of her subjects. Viewing her work makes me weep, as it is witnessing pure truth. Lori gifted me with permission to alter some of her powerful imagery for this book, and this project is one example of that.

The technique of hand-tinting daguerreotypes in the nineteenth century gave black-and-white portraits life-like appearances, while exuding a special charm in the process. You can replicate this old-fashioned technique with your own black-and-white and sepia-toned portraits by applying Solid Color Fill Layers to the photos.

WHAT YOU'LL NEED

DIGITAL MATERIALS

Subject photo: portrait

Texture photo: natural texture (such as a tree stump or wood surface)

Sources for project artwork

Black-and-white portrait: Lori Vrba (www.lorivrba.com)

Tree stump texture: www.textureking.com

TECHNICAL SKILLS

Duplicating a file (p. 15)

Feathering (p. 16)

Adding a Solid Color Fill Layer (p. 15)

Adjusting the Opacity of a layer (p. 12)

Selecting a foreground/background color (p. 10)

Creating a new layer (p. 10)

Merging layers/flattening an image (p. 11)

Adjusting Hue/Saturation (p. 12)

Apply the Gaussian Blur filter (p. 14)

Converting Background to Layer 0 (p. 10)

Arranging layers (p. 11)

Adjusting the blending mode of a layer (p. 12)

Moving a file into another (p. 9)

Resizing (p. 16)

Using Tools:

Lasso Tool (p. 9)

Brush Tool (p. 17)

Blur Tool (p. 17)

Crop Tool (p. 17)

Remove color and select face

Open your photo and duplicate the file. If your photo is not black and white, remove the color (ENHANCE>ADJUST COLOR>REMOVE COLOR). Then select the face by tracing around it with the Magnetic Lasso Tool. Feather the edges of this selection, setting the Feather Radius to 30 pixels. This will soften the harsh lines.

Add new fill layer of solid color to face

While the face is still selected, add a new fill layer with solid color. When the menu opens, use the default settings. Pick a skin tone color from the color menu. Then in the Layers Palette, set the Opacity level to 21%.

Add new fill layer of solid color to lips

Select the lips with the Magnetic Lasso Tool and feather the selection with a Radius of 30 pixels. Add a new fill layer to the lips as you did to the face in step 2. This time, choose a red color and set the Opacity to 3%. This slightly darkens the lips.

Add new fill layer of solid color to hair

Select the hair with the Magnetic Lasso Tool and feather the selection with a Radius of 30 pixels. (In my photo, the entire background is hair. To select both sides at once, I selected the background on one side of the face, pressed the Shift key and then selected the background on the other side.) Feather the edges of the selections with a Radius of 30 pixels. Then add a new fill layer of your desired solid color and then set the Opacity to 15%.

Enhance freckles with Brush Tool

To enhance features such as freckles or beauty marks, use the Brush Tool. Select brown as the foreground color (in the toolbar) and create a new layer. Chose a Hard Round Brush from the Default Brushes dropdown menu in the Brush Toolbar and set the Size to 5 pixels. "Paint" over individual freckles with a click of the mouse. In the Layers Palette, set the Opacity of the new layer to 22%.

Add new fill layer of solid color to cheeks

To add a bit of blush to the cheeks, use another solid color fill layer, this time in pink. I feathered the selection with a Radius of 30 pixels, and set the Opacity to 28%.

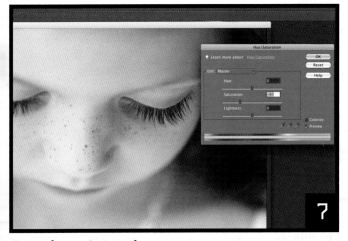

Tone down Saturation

Merge all the layers. Then tone down the Saturation of the entire piece, if desired, by going to the Adjust Hue/Saturation Menu. I set the Saturation to –40.

Apply Gaussian Blur Filter

Although I love the graininess of black-and-white photos produced from film, I thought this digital art needed a softer look to better accommodate the subtle colorization. To do the same in your working file, first duplicate the layer. Then apply the Gaussian Blur Filter to this new layer (which will automatically be selected). Set the Radius to 11.4 pixels.

Adjust blending mode to Darken

If you haven't already, convert the Background layer to Layer 0. Arrange the layers so the duplicated layer (Background copy) is behind the original layer (Layer 0). Set the blending mode of the Background copy layer to Darken. You will get a softer look overall. Notice that some of the details (eyelashes and freckles especially) will almost look like they are sketched.

Blur grainy areas and crop image

Select the Blur Tool. Adjust the Size as needed (probably around 75 pixels). I set the Strength to 35%. Click over grainy areas of the piece to blur them slightly. You will immediately notice softening. Continue to blur until you are satisfied with the results. Crop the image as desired. (I cropped the right side of the photo.)

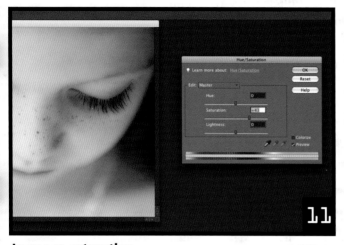

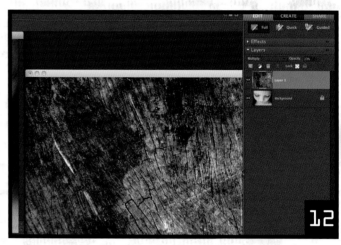

Increase saturation

As can sometimes happen, you might notice that your manipulations desaturated some of the colorizing work. It's just a quick fix to bring these colors back: Open the Hue/Saturation Menu and increase the Saturation as needed (I adjusted mine to +43).

Add texture photo and adjust blending mode

To add a hint of texture to the piece, open a photo of a natural texture (such as a tree stump). Move the texture to the working file. Adjust the size as needed to fit over the portrait. Set the blending mode of the texture layer to Multiply and adjust the Opacity to 13%. When the piece is complete, flatten the image and save the file.

▮Digital Detail

Because of its artistic quality, hand-tinting will enhance any portrait photo. However, to get the best results, it always helps to start with a great image. Here are some tips for getting good portrait photos:

- *Get familiar with your camera options and take practice shots to see what setting will work best for the shoot. Many digital cameras have portrait mode.*
- *The most flattering light for most portraits is soft and off-camera. Look for a large north-facing window if you're inside. If your subject is outdoors, an overcast day is best.*
- *To really capture subjects, let them be themselves. Subjects don't have to be smiling. Capturing unique expressions can result in beautiful photography.*
- *My favorite trick for good portraits is this: Get close and click away—even fill up your memory card if you need to. (My friend Lori, the photographer of the portrait used in this project, subscribes to the same thinking). If you get at least one or two great images out of the lot, it will have all been so worth it.*

LAURIE IN THE ORCHARD | BY SUSANNA GORDON

Originally, this image—taken on a spring day in a blossoming apple orchard with one of Susanna's dearest friends—was a black-and-white photo that she scanned into her computer. To add color, she applied a yellow solid fill layer at 20% Opacity. With the Brush Tool, set to a Soft Light blending mode, she applied several shades of green and yellow, varying the opacity and brush size. Overall, this gives a wonderful impression of traditional hand-painting on a printed photo.

CREDITS
Software: Adobe Photoshop 7

Technique to Try
Apply the color fill tinting method on a photo with a natural background, such as a garden.

AGLAOPE
Painting a Photo

■ Digital Detail

You can achieve more realistic painted effects by adding more than one layer of paint to areas of your photo. Keep the layers somewhat transparent (reduce the Opacity level) so that previous layers can peek through.

I have always had a fear of painting in the realist style. But Photoshop Elements is the perfect tool for helping me cope with this struggle, as it is a very forgiving medium, allowing me to delete and rework mistakes with the click of a button. When creating a digital painting, I like to start with either a photo or a sketch. Starting with a photo provides a framework that gives cues for where to block in color and create shadows and highlights. I digitally paint right onto the photo, which is a technique known as photo-painting. For me, this method provides a structure that is very freeing. Instead of anxiously looking at a blank page with pencil or brush in hand, I can jump right in and begin painting with confidence.

I highly recommend using a graphics tablet for this type of fine, repetitive work, both for better artistic results and to prevent injury. To give you an analogy: Can you imagine painting with an actual paintbrush that looks and performs like your mouse does? Didn't think so.

WHAT YOU'LL NEED

TECHNICAL SKILLS

Duplicating a file (p. 15)

Adjusting the Opacity of a layer (p. 12)

Selecting a foreground/background color (p. 10)

Adjusting Hue/Saturation (p. 12)

Adjusting Brightness/Contrast (p. 11)

Adjusting Color Curves (p. 11) (optional)

Loading a custom brush (p. 16)

Applying a Texturizer Filter (p. 15)

Using Tools:

Brush/Pencil Tool (p. 17)

Eraser Tool (p. 18) (optional)

Clone Stamp Tool (p. 17)

Color Replacement Tool (p. 17)

Eyedropper Tool (p. 18)

Lasso Tool (p. 9)

Burn/Dodge Tool (p. 17)

DIGITAL MATERIALS

Subject photo: portrait

Custom brush: shapes such as leaves or flowers

Custom brush: background, such as writing

Sources for project artwork

Leaf and text brushes: www. obsidiandawn.com

Block in white over skin tones

Open the portrait photo and duplicate it. This will be your working file. With the Brush Tool, paint a light color over the skin tones. Choose a brush from the Dry Media Brushes drop-down menu in the Brush Toolbar. I used the Pastel on Charcoal Paper 63. Adjust the Size of the brush as desired. I lowered the Opacity to 61% so that some of the features and shadows of the photo would show through. (Note: It's okay to be messy, as you can use the Eraser Tool to fix mistakes. Lower the Opacity level of the eraser for more subtle erasures.)

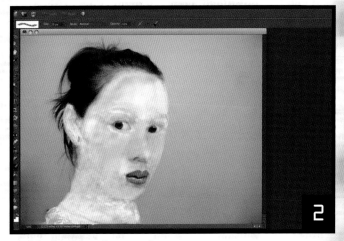

Add shadows in purple

Add shadows to the face and neck with dark lavender paint, using shadows on the original photo as a guide. Choose the Soft Mechanical 65 pixels brush from the Basic Brushes drop-down menu. I set the Size to 75 pixels. Choose a very low Opacity; I used 9%. Once you apply some shadows, go back and forth between applying a white base and lavender shadows until you are satisfied with the results.

■Digital Detail

I recommend creating a new layer for each set of brush and/or pencil detail. This will allow you to apply a blending mode or effect to a particular layer and adjust the Opacity level of the layer at a later point. If you are unhappy with a layer, you may choose to delete it.

For this project, I placed all details on the same layer. If I wanted to get rid of a recent error, all I had to do was go to Undo History (WINDOW>UNDO HISTORY) to delete it. In addition, if I find there are details I don't care for, I usually prefer to rework what I have (like I would in the actual studio) rather than delete and start from scratch. Of course, this is just my personal preference, so choose the method that works best for you.

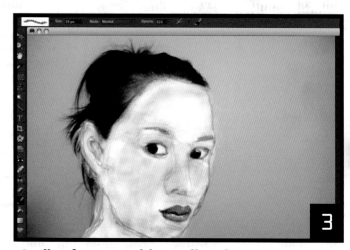

Outline features with Pencil Tool

Sketch in and outline the facial features with the Pencil Tool. Choose gray paint (to resemble pencil lead or charcoal) and the Hard Mechanical 9 pixels brush from the Basic Brushes drop-down menu. Set the Opacity low (I used 13%.) Then complete additional work on the neck, if needed.

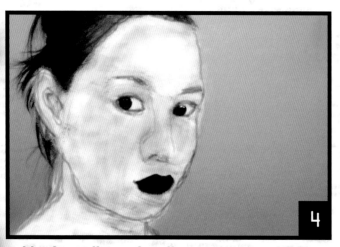

Add color to lips and outline

Now, block in the lip color using the Brush Tool. Set your foreground color as desired. I wanted the lips to stand out, so I chose a deep red color. Choose the Pastel on Charcoal Paper 63 pixels brush from the Dry Media Brushes drop-down menu. Adjust the Size and Opacity of the brush as needed. I set the Size to 19 pixels and Opacity to 61%. Add color to the lips. Then outline the lips as you did in step 3. I chose a dark gray paint with a slightly higher Opacity.

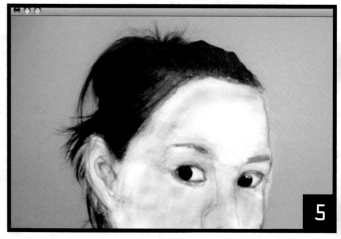

Color hair with Brush Tool

Using the Brush Tool, paint over the hair. Use the Pastel on Charcoal Paper 63 pixels brush from the Dry Media Brushes drop-down menu. Set your foreground color as desired. I selected reddish-brown paint first and then painted a second time with light brown paint. Adjust the Size and Opacity of your brush as needed. When you're finished, use the Pencil Tool as you did in step 3 to add texture to the hair. Using the same Dry Media Brush as before, add a transparent coat of white paint over the hair to soften and blend it with the composition (to make the paint transparent, lower the brush Opacity level).

Paint background

Select a color to paint in the background; I recommend using a similar color to the one you used to complete the shadows (in step 2) as it will give the piece a more cohesive look when the hue is adjusted in the next step. Select the Brush Tool and the Hard Mechanical 60 pixels brush from the Basic Brushes drop-down menu. Paint the background of the portrait using varying sizes and opacities of the brush to create a realistically painted look. I started with a Size of 210 pixels and Opacity at 38%.

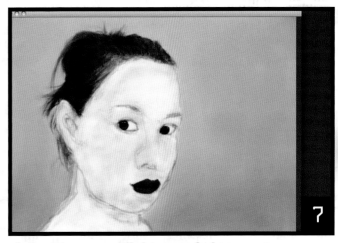

Adjust tones and lightness of piece

Now adjust the piece as a whole. You can change the Hue/Saturation, Brightness/Contrast and/or Color Curves until you achieve your desired results. Put any adjustments on a new adjustment layer.

Apply custom brushes to background

Load your custom brushes. (If you prefer, you can use one of the brushes in the drop-down menu in the Brush Toolbar.) I chose a handwritten brush and a leaf brush for an interesting background. Adjust both the Size and the Opacity of each brush as desired. For a subtle look, as I achieved, set the Opacity of the brushes to less than 30%. Then stamp the brushes in the background of the photo, being careful to avoid stamping the face.

Smooth lines in face

Remove some of the pencil sketches and other imperfections using the Clone Stamp Tool. Pick up some of the paint color on the face and copy it over the areas you want to remove. To help the cloning appear smooth, I usually set the Opacity of the tool to about 50%, and then adjust it from there as needed. I like to experiment with different brush types as well, but using the Hard Mechanical Brush is always a safe bet. When you're finished cloning, add more shadows to the face and neck as you did in step 2. Finally, add a light pink color to the cheeks using the Brush Tool. For a soft blush effect, choose the Soft Mechanical Brush from the Basic Brushes palette and lower the Opacity to 10–15%.

Adjust color of areas to blend

You may need to adjust the color of various areas to blend them in. I adjusted the hair color. An easy way to do this is to use the Color Replacement Tool with a large brush Diameter (about 70 pixels). I adjusted the settings as follows: Mode: Color; Limits: Contiguous; Tolerance: 30%. Use the Eyedropper Tool to select a color from your piece. (I chose purple-gray.) Then brush over the hair. You don't need to be careful around the edges because any areas that aren't the same color as the hair won't be changed.

Continue adjusting colors as needed

I reduced the overall tone of Yellows in the Hue/Saturation Menu. Then I also adjusted the color of the lips. To do so, select the lips using the Magnetic Lasso Tool and adjust the Hue/Saturation on a new adjustment layer. I increased the Lightness of the Reds to +43. To define the lips, add a bit of transparent white using white brushstrokes with a lowered Opacity to create highlights.

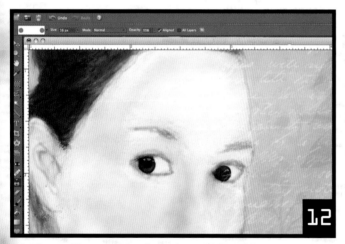

Clean up lines with Clone Stamp Tool

Use the Clone Stamp Tool (set to an Opacity of about 16%) to clean up some of the excess sketchy black lines around the eyes. Use the Clone Stamp Tool again to soften more of the excess outlines around the face and also to add more shadows. With the tool, pick up the flesh color to soften and/or clean up the outlines and pick up the purple shadow tone to create more shadows. Then continue to define the eyes by outlining them with the Pencil Tool, using black paint and the Hard Mechanical Brush set to 5 pixels and an Opacity of 9%. When outlining the eyes, go over the strokes a few times to achieve a sketched look.

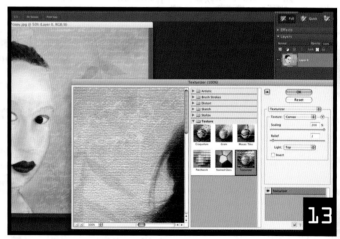

Apply Texturizer Filter

And now for a really fun part! Add a filter to make the painted piece look like it was rendered on canvas. Apply the Texturizer Filter and set the levels as follows: Texture: Canvas; Scaling: 200%; Relief: 2; Light: Top. Make any final adjustments as desired. I liked the more defined outlines I created in the face in step 3 and wanted to enhance those lines. An easy way to do that is with the Burn Tool. (I set the Range to Shadows and the Exposure to 20%.) Set the Burn Tool to a small size and brush over outlines and highlighted areas to inrease their intensity. To lighten spots, use the Dodge Tool. Save the file.

LETTING GO |
BY SUSAN MCKIVERGAN

Letting Go *was inspired by the idea of trying to let go of something you cannot have. The butterflies represent a sort of freedom—uncontainable, uncontrollable, as they morph out of the picture and come to life. The girl is overcome with great sadness and heartache, even in her brightly colored room, as she grieves for what she cannot have and must let go of it.*

Susan's piece was constructed from several different photos, which she merged and then painted over. Digitally painted elements include the girl, her hair, butterflies, the couch, and the poppies.

CREDITS
Software: Adobe Photoshop CS3

Technique to Try
Manipulate a digital photo using one or more of the techniques you've already learned. Then create a photo-painting from the altered image.

I heard barking deer in the middle of the night...thankfully I had been warned about how they sound. Jet lag is on my side and I find myself awake with the sunrise. So when we had to get up at four forty five for the Moonene Beach sunrise shoot I was game. I'd never shot the sunrise on a beach before, let alone in Hawaii. The sounds and smell assault my senses. Breathing in...

et into
m feeling
oloaki with
st talented
s in the
th as been
d inspired me
many amazing
things.

3

Pasting Pieces

Layering elements to create digital collages

The term collage means "to glue." Historically, it was used to describe the art of Pablo Picasso and Georges Braque and refers to a piece of artwork that combines separate images. Digital collage functions in much the same way, only the design elements are digital, such as scans or photographs and other elements like custom brushes and textures. The added bonus in creating a digital collage is that design elements used in your work can be tweaked to be exactly what you need—alter the size, shape, color and other tonal aspects of your elements, duplicate them or delete an element with the click of a button.

In this chapter, you will learn how to create pieces that artfully combine a variety of images through the use of layers and Opacity level adjustments, apply filters to alter tonal aspects of your work, add spotlight effects to highlight important design elements, create a purely digital scrapbook layout and more!

MY FLEDGLING
Merging Transparent Layers

This past summer my son became very comfortable with the ocean, no longer needing to hold my hand, going in knee-deep instead of cautiously brushing his toes against the foamy shore. With my camera, I captured him heading off to play in the sea, utterly independent, with red bucket in hand. As I looked through the lens, I experienced a defining moment —I could see that this was the beginning of letting go as a parent. Thus, this piece is titled *My Fledgling*.

In this digital collage, I imposed a photo of birds, imagery of an angel statue and a texture photo over the original photo of my son. I played with their Opacity levels to achieve a variety of transparent effects. The bird eating from the human hand is symbolic of motherhood and nurturing one's child. The second bird, imposed over my son, is the fledgling, symbolic of independence and wholeness. The imagery of the angel represents my son's guardian angel, who watches over him at all times, even when I am not with him.

WHAT YOU'LL NEED

TECHNICAL SKILLS

Duplicating a file (p. 15)

Adjusting Shadows/Highlights (p. 12)

Moving a file into another (p. 9)

Resizing/rotating (p. 16)

Adjusting the Opacity of a layer (p. 12)

Merging layers/flattening an image (p. 11)

Feathering (p. 16)

Adjusting Color Curves (p. 11)

Using Tools:

Lasso Tool (p. 9)

Eraser Tool (p. 18)

DIGITAL MATERIALS

Subject photo: a small subject in a large background

Two additional photos: one will be more prominent than the other, and photos with dark or black backgrounds work best

Texture photo

Sources for project artwork

Bird and angel photos: Lisa Solonynko (www.morguefile.com)

Texture: www.morguefile.com

Adjust Shadows/Highlights on subject photo

Open the subject photo. A photo with a small subject set in a large background works best for this project. I chose a subject photo of my son on the beach. Duplicate the file; this will be your working file. Play with shadow and highlight levels to give the photo some drama by going to the Shadows/Highlights Menu. I set my levels as follows: Lighten Shadows: 53%; Darken Highlights: 0%; Midtone Contrast: 100%.

Open and adjust secondary photo

Open the more prominent additional photo and move it into the working file. Resize it as needed to fit the working file. Set the Opacity level of this new layer to about 50%.

Merge layers and adjust Shadows/Highlights

Merge the layers. As needed, adjust the shadow and highlight levels. I felt my piece lacked intensity, so I adjusted the Shadows/Highlights to infuse it with a bit more electricity. Significantly increasing the contrast of the midtones helped me achieve this. I set the levels as follows: Lighten Shadows: 9%; Darken Highlights: 6%; Midtone Contrast: 100%.

Select and move object in third photo

Open the other secondary photo. A photo with a lot of contrast between the subject and background works best for this. Using the Magnetic Lasso Tool, trace around the subject of the photo. Feather the edges of the selection with a Radius of 5 pixels. Move the selection to the working file and resize it to fit. Set the Opacity of this new layer to 13%.

Adjust Color Curves and Hue/Saturation

Open the Color Curves Menu. Play with Shadows, Midtone Contrast, Midtone Brightness and Highlights by adjusting the sliders. Then, using the Magnetic Lasso Tool, select various areas of the working file and adjust the Hue/Saturation and Brightness/Contrast as desired.

Add texture photo

Open the texture photo and move it into the working file. Adjust the size as necessary to fit. Set the blending mode of the texture layer to Overlay and adjust the Opacity to 36%. Use the Eraser Tool (set to an Opacity of 20%) to erase the part of the texture layer that covers up the subjects in the photos. Here, I erased parts that covered up the angel statue. When the piece is complete, flatten the image and save the file.

NATURE'S GRAFFITI |
BY MARIE OTERO

Marie's piece is composed of multiple layers. The colored background and brick wall images are layered over imagery of a textured grain, with their Opacity settings reduced to allow for the elements of the wall and background color to show through. In addition, Marie applied different adjustment layers. The tree and weeds are created from two different photos that she manipulated with a Threshold New Adjustment Layer and an Outer Glow Layer Style with an Opacity of 75%.

CREDITS
Software: Adobe Photoshop CS4

Technique to Try
Experiment with different levels of Opacity and adjustment layers to achieve multiple looks using the same photo.

EN POINTE
Applying Filters: Invert and Poster Edges

The art of dance frequently makes its appearance in my artwork, as I am fascinated by the subject matter. When I dance to music, I often find myself performing ballet-like moves that seem ingrained, although I have never studied ballet (in this lifetime). I've often wondered if these are traces of a past life, if you believe in that kind of thing. I certainly cannot execute the moves with any kind of grace or technique, except maybe in my artwork.

Using the Invert Filter can result in dramatic effects, as it inverts all colors in an image. Applying this type of filter to an entire piece can sometimes achieve the look you want, but oftentimes it can be too dramatic. When this is the case, I like to impose the Invert Filter on one layer (or on just a few layers) to achieve a more subtle look for the piece.

WHAT YOU'LL NEED

DIGITAL MATERIALS

Background photo: texture with rust/grunge and letters, numbers or other markings

Subject photo: crop subject (to use just the legs or head) as desired

Texture photo

Sources for project artwork

Rusty background photo: fox-out (www.morguefile.com)

Ballerina photo: ©iStock-photo.com/wwing

TECHNICAL SKILLS

Duplicating a file (p. 15)

Converting Background to Layer 0 (p. 10)

Moving a file into another (p. 9)

Resizing/rotating (p. 16)

Adjusting the Opacity of a layer (p. 12)

Adjusting Brightness/Contrast (p. 11)

Merging layers/flattening an image (p. 11)

Adjusting Hue/Saturation (p. 12)

Adjusting the blending mode of a layer (p. 12)

Using Tools:

Crop Tool (p. 17)

Apply Invert Filter to background photo

Open the photo of the rusty background and duplicate it; this will be your working file. Convert the Background to Layer 0. To make a negative version of the image (where the colors are reversed to their opposites), apply the Invert Filter (FILTER>ADJUSTMENTS>INVERT). Here, my red and purple background turned to blue and green.

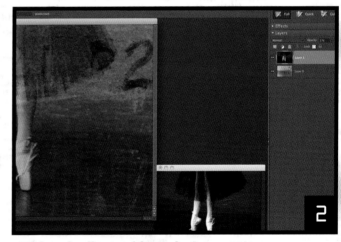

Add and adjust subject photo

Open the subject photo and move it into the working file (this photo will become Layer 1 and should be above Layer 0). Resize the layer to fit the background, and/or crop the file as needed. Set the Opacity of the subject layer to 57%.

Adjust Brightness/Contrast of subject layer

To make the subject pop a bit more, increase the brightness and contrast of Layer 1. In the Brightness/Contrast Menu, I set Brightness to 29 and Contrast to 63.

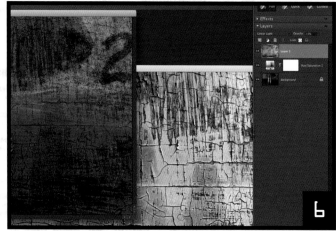

Apply Poster Edge filter

Merge all the layers. To add texture and depth to your image, apply the Poster Edges Filter (FILTER>ARTISTIC>POSTER EDGES). I set the levels as follows: Edge Thickness: 10; Edge Intensity: 0; Posterization: 6.

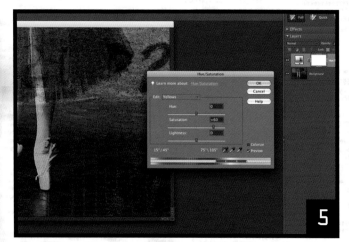

Adjust hues

It's always a good idea to step back and take a look at a piece to see what additional adjustments can benefit it. In fact, I came back to this piece at a later date, and was moved to make a couple of additions. To give your piece a warmer tone, increase the yellow hues. Open the Hue/Saturation Menu and make the changes in a new adjustment layer. In the Edit drop-down menu, select Yellows and change the Saturation to about +60.

Add and adjust texture photo

Open the texture photo and move it into the working file. Adjust the size as needed to fit the working file. Set the blending mode of the new layer (Layer 1) to Linear Light and adjust the Opacity to 17%. Flatten the image and save the file.

LOST AND FOUND |
BY PEGGI MEYER GRAMINSKI

Lost and Found *represents hope. Even when we are faced with a problem we deem hopeless, the key to its resolution is often nearby, sometimes right under our feet. The stars in the night sky represent an unyielding element of hope even when our current position appears bleak.*

Peggi combined two color photos in this piece. She utilized the invert function in Corel Paint Shop Pro on a photo she took outside of Bisbee, Arizona (of the grass and trees). She softened areas of the photo, colorizing it a bit here and there, and, finally, she added the finishing touches—the key and the stars in a black night sky.

CREDITS
Software: Corel Paint Shop Pro X

Technique to Try
Invert the color of just one area of a piece. Select an area with the Lasso Tool and then apply the Invert Filter to the selection.

HOPE AT ROCK BOTTOM
Applying Filters: Photo and Lighting Effects

When I create art, I often visit dark emotions. However, my work never seems to dwell in these places. There is almost always a sense of hope and a reaching toward the light in the subject matter. This piece is a very good example of what I am talking about.

Imposing a Photo Filter on your piece or on an aspect of your piece can change its overall color scheme, making the colors either warmer or cooler. Adding the Spotlight Filter creates an interesting lighting effect, and in this piece makes it look like there is light shining on the subject from above, beckoning the youngster out of rock-bottom. Applying blending modes to filter layers can generate further interesting results. I recommend trying out a variety of filter settings and blending modes, as each one creates a different effect, and you are bound to find more than one that works really well with your piece.

WHAT YOU'LL NEED

TECHNICAL SKILLS

Duplicating a file (p. 15)

Applying the Photo Filter (p. 15)

Adjusting the blending mode of a layer (p. 12)

Moving a file into another (p. 9)

Arranging layers (p. 11)

Resizing/rotating (p. 16)

Feathering (p. 16)

Applying the Lighting Effects Filter (p. 14)

Merging layers/flattening an image (p. 11)

Using Tools:

Magic Wand Tool (p. 9)

Lasso Tool (p. 9)

DIGITAL MATERIALS

Painted background: you can use a photo or scan in your own painting

Subject photo: works best with a solid background

Additional subject photo

Texture photo: rough texture

Sources for project artwork

Photo of mannequin: Clarita (www.morguefile.com)

Distressed wood texture: badeend (www.morguefile.com)

Photo of dove: ©iStockphoto.com/DNY59

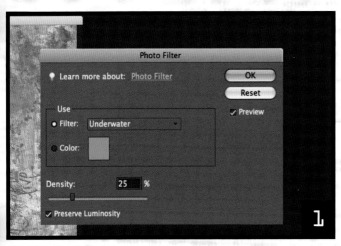

Apply Photo Filter to painted background

Open the painted background and make a duplicate of the file; this will be your working file. Then apply the Photo Filter on a new adjustment layer. Leave the mode at Normal and the Opacity at 100%. (These settings can be changed in the Layers Palette after the filter is applied.) Experiment with the various options in the Photo Filter Menu. I settled on Underwater, the default color (aqua) and a Density of 100%, and I checked the box for Preserve Luminosity.

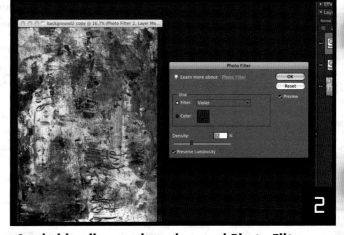

Apply blending mode and second Photo Filter

Experiment with various blending modes in the Layers Palette. I chose Multiply with 100% Opacity. Adjust the color further by applying another photo filter. For a bit less green, apply the Photo Filter again using the following settings: Filter: Violet (default color); Density: 32%; Check the box for Preserve Luminosity.

Add subject photo and remove background

Open the photo with the primary subject. (A photo with a solid [or nearly solid] background works best.) Move it into the working file and make sure the layer is on top of the painted background. Set the blending mode to Hard Light—this will allow the painted background to show through. Then, with the Magic Wand Tool set to a Tolerance of about 10, select the background area of the subject photo and delete it. Position the subject as desired. Here, my subject is near the bottom to give him the feel of being at the bottom of an enclosed space.

Add and adjust rough texture photo

Open the rough texture photo (here, I used a photo of distressed wood) and move it into your working file. Resize it to fit the working file. Set the blending mode of this new layer to Hard Light, which will give the effect of adding highlights to the image. Move the texture layer behind the subject layer.

Apply spotlight filter

Apply a spotlight to the rough texture layer by going to the Lighting Effects Filter Menu. Here, I set the levels as follows: Style: Soft Spotlight; Light Type: Spotlight; Intensity: Negative 98 and Narrow 100; Focus: 100. Set the Properties as follows: Gloss: 0; Material: 75; Exposure: –36; Ambiance: 15; Texture Channel: None; Height: 50.

Add and adjust second subject photo

Open the second subject photo. With the Magnetic Lasso Tool, trace around the subject to select it. Feather the edges of the selection with a Radius of 30. Move the selection into the working file and place it as desired. Resize and rotate the layer as needed. Set the blending mode of this new layer to Hard Light. Flatten the image and save the file.

VIRTUE | BY GALE BLAIR

For this piece, Gale wanted to create something with a dreamy quality, like looking through a mist. She prefers artwork that is more figurative than literal, in which emotions are expressed. "That's what I hoped to achieve with my piece," she says.

Gale used a Cooling Filter set to a Density of 37%. She applied the Difference blending mode to the filter, which toned down the contrast of the background image. To bring out the warm tones in her collage and take out a bit of the blue cast on the figure's face, she used a Deep Red Filter set to a Density of 24%.

CREDITS
Software: Adobe Photoshop CS3

Technique to Try
Create a digital collage using a Photo Filter setting you haven't tried before.

GO FREE
Creating with Scrapbook Kits

go free

heart wide open

I remember the first time I saw a digitally rendered scrapbook page in a popular magazine. My jaw dropped as I thought, "How could this be digital?" Every element in the design appeared so realistic, from the ephemera used, which had a three-dimensional effect, to the inked edges of the linen paper. I quickly became hooked on creating art with digital scrapbook kits. The elements contained in digital scrapbooking kits are perfect not only for digital scrapbook layouts but also for digital collages. There is a plethora of these products online; if you can find it in an actual scrapbooking store, you can also find a digital version.

WHAT YOU'LL NEED

DIGITAL MATERIALS

Subject photo

Digital scrapbook paper: a background paper and another paper (in strips or whole) (Note: You can purchase a scrapbook kit or buy elements individually)

Digital frame embellishment

Small digital embellishment, like a flower or heart

Digital scrapbook letters (individual letter files)

Digital tags or tabs

Sources for project artwork

Digital kit: Urban Bohemian by Jen Wilson Designs (www.jenwilsondesigns.com)

Font: 1942 Report font (www.dafont.com)

TECHNICAL SKILLS

Duplicating a file (p. 15)

Selecting a foreground/background color (p. 10)

Moving a file into another (p. 9)

Resizing/rotating (p. 16)

Converting Background to Layer 0 (p. 10)

Arranging layers (p. 11)

Merging layers/flattening an image (p. 11)

Duplicating a layer (optional) (p. 10)

Using Tools:

Magic Wand Tool (p. 9)

Marquee Tool (p. 18)

Paint Bucket Tool (p. 18)

Brush Tool (p. 17)

Type Tool (p. 18)

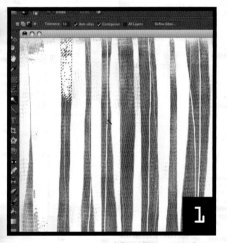

1

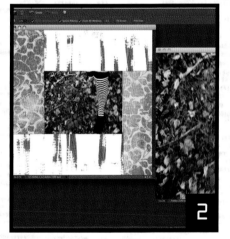

2

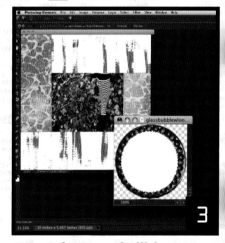

3

Remove areas of background paper

Open the digital paper file that will be your background and duplicate it. This will be your working file. To give the paper a grungy, distressed appearance, obliterate parts of the pattern. Set the background color to white and then use the Magic Wand Tool, set to a Tolerance of 50, to select a random area of the pattern. Then press the Delete key. Repeat to remove areas all over the paper.

Add photo and strips of paper

Open your personal photo and move it into the working file. Resize it as desired and center it on the background, leaving a wide frame around the photo. Open a strip of digital paper and move it into your working file. (If you do not have a strip of digital paper, simply select a rectangular area from a full-sized digital paper and move the selection to your working file.) Duplicate this layer to create a second strip, and place it as desired.

Create frame embellishment

Open the digital frame. Use the Marquee Tool to create a shape slightly larger than the transparent part of the frame. Select white as the foreground color, then select the Paint Bucket Tool. Click on the shape to fill it with white. Deselect it. Make sure the Background layer is changed to Layer 0, then arrange the layers so that the shape is behind the frame. Open a small digital element and move it into the file with the frame and arrange it behind the frame. Flatten the layers and then move it into the working file.

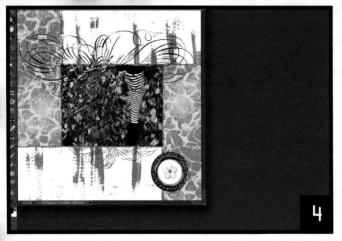

Add additional elements

Open the files with additional embellishments and move them into the working file, placing them as desired. Here, I placed stitches along the edges of the photo and the strips of paper. I also added flourishes to frame the photo.

Add title letters

To add the title text to your piece, open up the appropriate letter files. (Each letter is its own image file.) Move the letters into the working file, place them as desired, and rotate and resize them. Merge the layers.

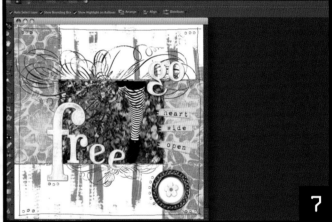

Draw frame and doodles

Add hand-drawn doodles to your piece. Select the Brush Tool and choose Calligraphic Brushes. Choose the Flat Brush 7 pixels from the menu. Keep the default settings. Use this brush to draw a rough frame around the piece, and also doodle in other areas as desired. To create small, circular doodles, choose the Circle 1 18 pixels brush from the Assorted Brushes Menu and set it to 49 pixels with a Dissolve Mode.

Add tags and type text

Open the file with the tag and move it into the working file. Resize and rotate it as desired; you will add text to the tag, so make sure it is large enough for type. Duplicate the layer as needed for additional text. Select the Horizontal Type Tool and click on your tag. Type your text as desired. Then select the Move Tool and rotate the type layer to fit the tag. Repeat to add text to other tags. When the piece is complete, flatten the image and save the file.

■Digital Detail

These sites are just a few of the many with
a range of digital scrapbook kits:
www.oscraps.com
www.wearestorytellers.com
www.littledreamerdesigns.com

MOLOKIA | BY MICHELLE SHEFVELAND

"The intent of this piece was to create a journal of my magical photography trip to Hawaii, so I included an open sketchbook, journaling from my trip, various ephemera and favorite images from my journey," says Michelle. She applied various blending modes, used imagery of hand-painted paper and utilized digital brushwork. Michelle created custom lifted shadows on many of the elements using the Warp Tool (which is available in Photoshop). To subdue their intensity, she gave the photos a sepia tint.

CREDITS
Supplies: Nature's Sketchbook (Journals 1, Papers 2 [background], Ivy League Pak [staples], Nature's Garden Element Pak (bee sticker, hinge), Keys 2 My Heart Pak (key string), Peaceful Moments Pak (vintage frames) by Michelle Shefveland (www.cottagearts.net); Scarlet Memoirs Page Pak (postcard), Destinations Pak (flourish), Golden Autumn Pak (old farmer's almanac) by Doris Castle (www.cottagearts.net); Manila Picks Pak (postcards, ticket, vintage program) by Julie Mead (www.cottagearts.net); It's my History Kit (herbs) in Learning Digital Scrapbooking with PSE7 training CD (www.cottagearts.net)
Fonts: Hawaii Killer, Jefferson, Typical Writer
Software: Adobe Photoshop CS3

Technique to Try
To add more depth to your digital kit elements, add a drop shadow to each layer. To do so, open the Effects Palette, click on the Layer Styles icon, select Drop Shadows from the drop-down menu, and choose the low or soft edge drop shadow option. To adjust the shadow, double-click on the "fx" in the Layers Palette.

SELF-PORTRAIT
Creating a Self-Portrait Collage

The creation of a self-portrait can be an opportunity for self-discovery, not only physically but also emotionally and even spiritually. A self-portrait is documentation of who we are at a particular point in our lives. Some artists search for answers about themselves through the act of self-portraiture, while others use it as a form of self-expression to reveal what they already know about themselves. The process of creating a self-portrait can be cathartic and healing. Within the layers of our likeness depicted through our art, we can see where we have come from and where we now stand, and we can project our intentions of who we would like to become. For this project, try combining imagery of yourself with other photos or elements of photos that have strong personal meaning. See where the process leads you and how it can change you, for the better.

WHAT YOU'LL NEED

DIGITAL MATERIALS

Photo of yourself: photo should just be of your face and neck

Additional photo: something from nature, such as a tree or flowers, works well

Texture photo

Sources for project artwork

Photo of tree: www.morguefile.com

TECHNICAL SKILLS

Creating a new blank file (p. 8)

Moving a file into another (p. 9)

Arranging layers (p. 11)

Adjusting the blending mode of a layer (p. 12)

Adjusting the Opacity of a layer (p. 12)

Merging layers/flattening an image (p. 11)

Using Tools:

Magic Wand Tool (p. 9)

Brush Tool (p. 17)

Clone Stamp Tool (p. 17)

Crop Tool (p. 17)

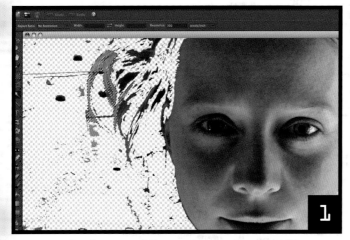

Remove background from photo of yourself

Open the photo of yourself. Then create a new blank file, selecting Transparent as the Background Contents and making the measurements the same as those for the photo of yourself. (Go to IMAGE>RESIZE to check those measurements.) Set the Color Mode to RGB Color. This will be your working file. Move the photo of yourself into the working file. Use the Magic Wand Tool to delete the areas surrounding your face (like the background and your hair). Using the Magic Wand Tool (instead of the Lasso Tool) will give the piece a distressed look. Play with the Tolerance level setting as needed.

Add additional photo behind your photo

Set the blending mode to Hard Light. Open the additional photo and move it into the working file (it will become Layer 2). Resize it to fit the working file. Then arrange the layers so the new photo is behind the photo of yourself.

Stamp grunge brush in new layer

Select the Brush Tool and set the foreground color as desired. Open the Default Brushes Menu. Select the Rough Round Bristle Brush (#100). (Instead, you can load a new grunge brush; see page 16 to learn how.) Set the Opacity to about 40% and adjust the Size to slightly larger than the default. Before stamping with your brush, create a new layer for the brushwork. Stamp the brush over the area where the nature image is.

Change blending mode of Layer 2

When your brushwork is finished, move the layer (which should be Layer 3) behind Layer 2. Set the blending mode of Layer 3 to Hard Mix, and play with the Opacity until you are satisfied. Merge the layers.

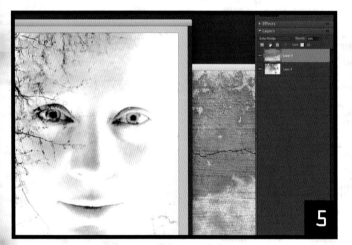

Add and adjust texture photo

Open the texture photo. Move the texture photo to your working file and resize it to fit as needed. Set the blending mode of the layer to Color Dodge (which brightens the base color), and the Opacity to 48%. Merge the layers.

Remove hard edges with Clone Stamp Tool

Using the Clone Stamp Tool you can get rid of the hard edges on the left and right sides of the face. Just clone the texture that you want instead (like the light background), and lay it down over the hard edges. Also use the Clone Stamp Tool to remove dark, spotty areas in the working file. Clone the light areas around the dark spots to cover them. To help the cloning appear smooth, I usually set the Opacity of the tool to about 50% and then adjust it from there as needed. When you're finished cloning, crop the working file if desired. Save the file when you're done.

UNTITLED | BY JULIA VAN DER WERF

"While making this self-portrait I learned what a patient person I am," she says. "It takes hours to find the right elements and colors. I start over again and again until I am satisfied with the result." Julia used several images to create the foreground of this self-portrait piece and painted four of the layers with the Airbrush Tool. Julia says the secret to this piece is transparency. She erased part of each layer to let the layers beneath show through. She applied a Threshold Filter to the imagery of herself. The imagery of the window is an element from one of her own digital scrapbook kits.

CREDITS
Software: Corel Paint Shop Pro

Technique to Try

Combine three or more images in a self-portrait.

WALTER'S BROKEN HEART
Colorizing With the Brush Tool

I collect vintage photos and have a fondness for cabinet cards and tintypes. The absence of expression on the faces of subjects in these old photos intrigues me because even though the people are striking stone-cold poses, their true essences always seem to shine through, usually in their eyes. It fascinates me when I can see a smile in the eyes or a sadness in the posture. I enjoy trying to capture these essences in digital pieces, like I did in this piece.

In *Veruca's Dream* (on page 50), I replicated the traditional art of tinting photos with the use of Solid Color Fill Layers. In this project, you'll learn to simulate the same process through a different approach—using the Brush Tool. Photoshop Elements provides many Brush options and settings, allowing for exactly your desired results.

DIGITAL MATERIALS

Environment photo: an open environment, such as an empty room or a clearing in a field

Texture photo: cracked texture

Texture photo: vintage texture

Subject photo: black-and-white photo; a vintage portrait works well, but you can also convert a color photo

Additonal photo: a frame; works best with a solid background and solid area inside the frame

Additonal photo: an image that will be framed

Additonal photo: a heart, either the organ or the shape

Custom brush: flame

Sources for project artwork

Photo of vintage gentleman: book CD

Cracked texture: www.morguefile.com

Photo of room: ©iStockphoto.com/gremlin

Photo of frame: ©iStockphoto.com/winterling

Photo of heart: clarita (www.morguefile.com)

Vintage texture: WHEREISHERE (www.flickr.com/groups/textures4layers)

TECHNICAL SKILLS

Duplicating a file (p. 15)

Moving a file into another (p. 9)

Resizing/rotating (p. 16)

Adjusting the blending mode of a layer (p. 12)

Adjusting the Opacity of a layer (p. 12)

Arranging layers (p. 11)

Selecting a foreground/background color (p. 10)

Converting Background to Layer 0 (p. 10)

Loading a custom brush (p. 16)

Using the Effects Palette (p. 14)

Adjusting Hue/Saturation (p. 12)

Duplicating a layer (p. 10)

Merging layers/flattening an image (p. 11)

Using Tools:

Lasso Tool (p. 9)

Magic Wand Tool (p. 9)

Eraser Tool (p. 18)

Zoom Tool (p. 18)

Brush Tool (p. 17)

Blur Tool (p. 17)

Clone Stamp Tool (p. 17)

1

2

Duplicate environment and add texture

Open the environment photo and duplicate the file. This will be your working file. Here, I used a photo of a room as my background environment. Open the texture photo and move it into the working file. Resize as needed to fit the file. Set the blending mode of the texture layer to Vivid Light, and change the Opacity to 22%.

Select subject

Open the black-and-white subject photo and select the subject using the Magnetic Lasso Tool. Move the selection to the working file. Then use the Magic Wand and/or Eraser Tool to clean up the edges of the subject, removing any unwanted pixels. Use the Magic Wand Tool to select unwanted areas. Adjust the Tolerance as needed—the higher the Tolerance, the more pixels will be selected. Use the Eraser Tool to erase any unwanted areas. Zoom in while erasing for the most precise work.

Colorize black-and-white photo layer

Set the foreground color as desired. (If I'm colorizing a person, I prefer
to start with the skin. Here, I set the foreground to dark tan.) Select the
Brush Tool and choose the Hard Round Brush from the Default Brushes
Menu. Lower the Opacity to about 4%, and adjust the Size. Decrease the
Hardness of the brush (to aid in blending) by opening the drop-down
menu under the brush icon in the Brush Toolbar. For the hair, I started
with yellow and added brown on top to give the feel of actual hair with
various highlights.

Make frame transparent and add to file

Open the photo of the frame (you'll want a frame on a solid background). Change the Background layer to Layer 0. Then select the solid
background in the photo with the Magic Wand Tool. Delete the selection.
Move the frame into the working file. (The frame should be transparent.)

▮Digital Detail

*It's a good idea to put brushwork on a new
layer (LAYER>NEW>LAYER). This will allow
you to easily correct mistakes without dis-
turbing the rest of the piece.*

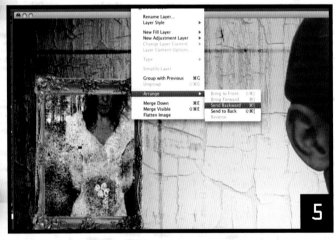

Arrange layers to frame photo

Open the photo that will be framed. Move it into the working file,
placing it over the frame. Arrange the layers so that this newest layer
is behind the frame layer (but still in front of the background layers).
Resize and rotate both layers as needed to fit them together.

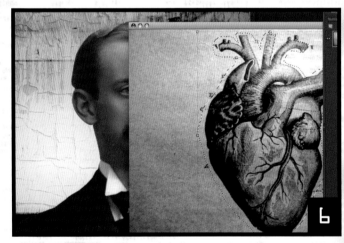

Add heart layer

Open the photo of the heart. Select it with the Magnetic Lasso Tool and
move it into the working file. Resize and rotate the layer as needed.
Clean up the edges with the Eraser Tool and/or Magic Wand Tool.

Split heart layer in half

To create the "broken" heart, choose the Polygonal Lasso Tool. Select half of the heart, making a zigzag pattern down the middle. Then move the selected area over to separate it.

Stamp custom brush flames

Adding flames to the piece enhances the symbolism of the broken heart. To add flames, first create a new layer (LAYER>NEW>LAYER) and set the foreground color to orange. (Putting brushwork on multiple layers will make it easier to change later.) Load the custom flame brush. (I played with the Size and Opacity of the brush until I was satisfied.) Stamp the flame on the new layer, and move the layer over the heart. Then arrange the layers so the flame layer is behind the heart layer. Then do the same to add flames to the frame. When you're finished, use the Eraser Tool to clean up any unwanted flames (or simply delete the layer).

Add drop shadows to subject and frame

Add drop shadows to both the subject layer and the frame layer. Click on the layer you want to add the shadow to, and go to the Effects Palette. Choose Drop Shadows in the drop-down menu and double-click on Soft Shadow. You can adjust the drop shadow by double-clicking on the "fx" icon on that layer in the Layers Palette.

Add and adjust vintage texture

Open the vintage texture layer and move it to your working file. Resize it as needed, and make sure this layer is at the front. Set the blending mode to Multiply.

Adjust hue of environment layer

Adjust the hue of the first layer (the environment, which is Layer 0). In the Hue/Saturation Menu, adjust Hue as desired. I moved the Hue slider to the left to get a greener hue.

Duplicate subject layer to lighten

To make the subject brighter, duplicate the layer. Set the blending mode of the duplicated layer to Hard Light.

Soften edges of subject layer

Merge the layers. Use the Blur Tool to soften the edges of the subject.

Make final adjustments

Make final adjustments to the piece as needed. Here, I added depth by making adjustments in the Brightness/Contrast Menu. I also decided that the shadow on the right side of the man's face was too intense and did not make sense given the light source. I used the Clone Stamp Tool to clone areas just outside the shadow and stamped them over the shadow. When you're finished, flatten the image and save the file.

THE FRUIT VASE |

BY RICHARD SALLEY

Richard's piece here has a total of 21 layers. The original image was in black and white. He created eight separate layers of color (orange, purple, yellow, light green, leaf green, brown, gold and red) and applied a Layer Mask (available in Photoshop). Masks enable you to hide portions of a layer and reveal the layers below.

CREDITS
Software: Adobe Photoshop CS2

Technique to Try

Replicate the masking technique discussed above using the Eraser Tool. First, colorize your photo using various layers of colors. To reveal bottom layers, erase areas of top layers using the Eraser Tool set to a low Opacity (less than 20%).

4

Seamlessly Blending

Merging images to create montage art

In his book, *Photoshop Collage Techniques,* Gregory Haun talks about the difference between collage and montage. In collage, separate elements usually have distinct lines and edges, making it easy to distinguish between the various components. Montage (sometimes referred to as photomontage) was used to define later works by artists like Max Ernst, who combined engravings, creating relatively seamless images. Montage is sometimes referred to as a form of collage; however, it has a distinct difference. In a montage, the separate images go together seamlessly, without the distinct edges that are present in collage. When looking at a digital montage, it is as if you are looking at a single photo, except you know that it's not possible, because the content is usually surreal.

Photoshop Elements provides numerous tools that aid in creating perfectly seamless digital montages—like various lighting effects, tools for applying shadows and, of course, blending modes. If you have ever dreamed of flying through the night sky tethered to a red, heart-shaped balloon, your dream can now come true.

I try to stay abreast of current events, but I have trouble watching the news on a daily basis, as I take so many things I hear to heart, often becoming depressed by what I watch. The amount of issues and problems we face as a nation and as a world can seem insurmountable, and I am often left questioning whether or not we can overcome. This piece is a representation of my questioning.

You can create custom brushes from a variety of sources, like selections of photographs, text you type and designs you create in Photoshop Elements, or scans of your doodles. Once the image is defined as a brush, it becomes a black-and-white image in your Brush Menu. Because creating montage involves a need for some realism, being able to make your own custom brushes is incredibly useful.

WHAT YOU'LL NEED

TECHNICAL SKILLS

DIGITAL MATERIALS

Additional photo: flames

Environment photo: you will add flames and smoke to this photo

Custom brush: smoke

Subject photo: black and white and with a solid black background; the environment photo will take this shape

Sources for project artwork

Photo of flame: by fattymatty-brewing (www.morguefile.com)

Photo of green building: by kevinrosseel (www.morguefile.com)

Photo of bucket: ©iStockphoto.com/agehret

Smoke brushes: by Graphics by _charon (http://ch-photo-shopped.livejournal.com/)

Feathering (p. 16)

Creating a new blank file (p. 8)

Moving a file into another (p. 9)

Duplicating a file (p. 15)

Selecting a foreground/background color (p. 10)

Creating a new layer (p. 10)

Loading a custom brush (p. 16)

Resizing/rotating (p. 16)

Adjusting the blending mode of a layer (p. 12)

Adjusting Hue/Saturation (p. 12)

Merging layers/flattening an image (p. 11)

Using Tools:

Marquee Tool (p. 18)

Lasso Tool (p. 9)

Crop Tool (p. 17)

Brush/Pencil Tool (p. 17)

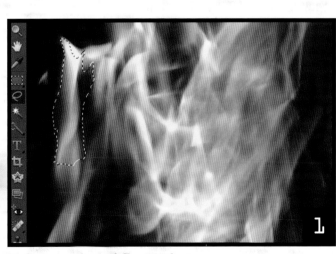

Select portion of flame photo
Open the photo of flames. With either the Marquee Tool or the Lasso Tool (which I used), select the portion of the photo you want to make into the brush shape. I extracted a portion of the fire, making sure to create a flame-like shape with the Lasso Tool. Feather the edges of the selection with a Radius of 10–20 pixels.

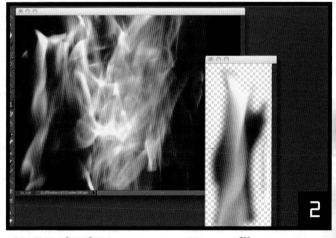

Move selection to new transparent file
Create a new blank file with a Color Mode set to RGB Color, 300 dpi and Background Contents Transparent. I sized the document to be 1000 × 1000 pixels, which gave me enough space to work in. Move your brush selection (from step 1) to the blank file. Crop the file as needed so it fits just around the brush.

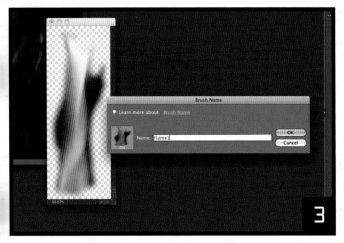

3

Define new file as a brush

Select the Brush Tool and then go to the set of brushes you want to add your custom brush to. I generally save my custom brushes to the Default Brushes set. To do this, just select Default Brushes in the Brush Toolbar. Then go to EDIT>DEFINE BRUSH. Name your brush and click OK. Your brush will appear at the bottom of the Default Brushes drop-down menu. Now you can use it like any other brush, choosing a size and color for it as you wish. I created three more flame custom brushes in the same manner.

4

Stamp brush onto environment photo

Open the environment photo and duplicate it. This will be your working file. Change the foreground color to orange and make sure your flame brush is still selected. Stamp flames on your photo. (I used a photo of a building and added flames to the windows.) To achieve a realistic look, try overlapping the different flames and playing with the Size and Opacity of the flame brushes you have created. It's also a good idea to put the brushwork on new layers so you can edit as needed.

5

Load and stamp smoke brush

To further the realism of the flames, load a custom brush of smoke. Select the brush and select gray as the foreground color. Play with the Opacity and Size. Then stamp the smoke brush. While stamping, consider the location of the smoke. I wanted all the smoke to look like it was moving in the same direction, as if blown by the wind.

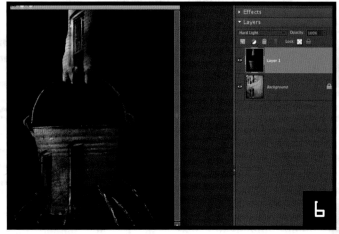

6

Add subject photo and adjust blending mode

Open the black-and-white subject photo; a photo with a black background will work best for this. Move this photo into the working file, and resize as needed to fit. Set the blending mode of this new layer to Hard Light. Adjust the Hue/Saturation of the final piece as desired. I adjusted the Hue of the Greens by increasing the Saturation to +128 (which changed the color to blue to emulate water). Flatten the image and save the file.

MYTH INTERPRETED |

BY KELLY SHERIDAN

Kelly designed Myth Interpreted *to depict the myth of Pandora. Her piece, in which Pandora sleeps upon a bed of words over an image of water, is made up of a variety of custom brushes that Kelly created in Photoshop. All of the text elements are custom brushes created from old book scans. The swirly images that float up from the open box are custom brushes as well.*

CREDITS
Software: Adobe Photoshop 7, Corel Painter 8

Technique to Try

Before stamping with a custom brush, set the blending mode to one of the Light selections (e.g., Soft Light, Hard Light, Vivid Light, etc.).

THE CHASE
Producing Motion with Blur Effects

Sometimes I visit difficult experiences in my work, in hopes of bringing them into the light and healing them. In this piece, I originally intended to explore the notions of fear and worry and how one can sometimes feel as if they are being chased relentlessly by these feelings. Something magical happened on my creative journey: I added the butterfly at the last minute, and it completely changed the mood of the piece. It went from the scary, desperate feeling of being chased to the endearing spirit of chasing a sweet butterfly.

The blur filters in Photoshop Elements are indispensable when it comes to creating movement in your artwork. Experiment with them, as each one will create a unique effect. You can further tweak each application by playing with the available settings. I wanted to make the female figure in this piece appear as if she were running, and I found that the Motion Blur Filter was best suited for achieving this effect.

WHAT YOU'LL NEED

DIGITAL MATERIALS

Environment photo: outdoor environment, such as a forest

Subject photo: a person (or animal) walking or running

Additional photo: object for subject to chase

Sources for project artwork

Photo of forest: Manina (www.morguefile.com)

Photo of woman: ©iStockphoto.com/mlenny

Photo of butterfly: ©iStockphoto.com/ranzino

TECHNICAL SKILLS

Duplicating a file (p. 15)

Moving a file into another (p. 9)

Resizing/rotating (p. 16)

Applying the Motion Blur Filter (p. 14)

Merging layers/flattening an image (p. 11)

Adding a Solid Color Fill Layer (p. 15)

Adjusting Color Curves (p. 11)

Duplicating a layer (p. 10)

Appling the Gaussian Blur Filter (p. 14)

Converting Background to Layer 0 (p. 10)

Arranging layers (p. 10)

Adjusting the Opacity of a layer (p. 12)

Using Tools

Lasso Tool (p. 9)

Magic Wand Tool (p. 9)

Eraser Tool (p. 18)

Zoom Tool (p. 18)

Open background photo and select subject
Open the photo of the outdoor environment and make a duplicate of the file; this will be your working file. Also open the photo of the moving subject. Using the Magnetic Lasso Tool, select the subject. Move the selection into the working file, placing and resizing it as you wish. Remove any unwanted areas around the edges of the selection. You can use the Magic Wand or Eraser tools to do so. Zoom in on the selection to achieve the most precise work.

Apply Motion Blur Filter to subject
To simulate motion, you need to apply the Motion Blur Filter on the layer with the subject (Layer 1). Set the Angle to 51 and Distance to 29 pixels. Merge the layers.

Add color fill layer to background

Adding a color to the background layer will allow you to create a mood for the piece. Here, purple makes for a quiet, eerie mood. Add a new Solid Color Fill Layer with your color of choice. Set the blending mode to Linear Burn and Opacity to 100%. Merge the layers.

Adjust tonal range

To adjust the tonal range of the working file, go to the Adjust Color Curves Menu. Here, I left the sliders alone and chose Increase Contrast in the Select a Style Menu.

Apply Gaussian Blur Filter

You should now have just one layer. Duplicate the layer. Apply the Gaussian Blur Filter to the layer copy. When the Gaussian Blur Menu is open, set the Radius to 3 pixels. Before you perform the next part of this step, make sure the original background layer (not the copy layer) is changed to Layer 0. Arrange the layers so the copy layer is behind the original layer (Layer 0). Reduce the Opacity of the original layer to 26%.

Add object to chase

Now add something for your subject to chase. Here, I added a butterfly. A photo with a solid background works best for this step. Open the photo and select the solid background with the Magic Wand Tool. Invert the selection (SELECT>INVERSE). Move the object into the working file and place, resize and rotate it as needed. Then apply the Motion Blur Filter to the object layer, and adjust the settings as desired. When the piece is complete, flatten the image and save the file.

THE RAVEN | BY TIFFINI ELEKTRA X

In this piece, Tiffini used the Blur Tool sparingly, but effectively, to make the background elements cohesive. She applied the Blur Tool to the background behind the raven in the circle as well as in some of the elements of the blue background. In addition, Tiffini applied a color fill and drop shadows and used the Burn/Dodge tools, and she created a few brushes like the white flowers and branches.

CREDITS
Software: Adobe Photoshop CS4

Technique to Try
Apply blur effects to the background of a piece rather than the subject. This will mimic the effect of a photo taken with the action setting.

TRAVEL LIGHT
Creating Shadows with the Burn Tool

Have you ever dreamed that you could fly? I find that my wildest dreams can come true when I create digital art. Not only can I fly, but I can also visit magical worlds, time travel and explore an endless number of possibilities in altered realities.

In order to create a believable digital montage it is necessary to create shadows that make sense given the light source. Photoshop Elements offers a variety of ways to make this happen, like adding drop shadows in the Effects Palette (as you used in *Walter's Broken Heart* on page 84) and using the Burn Tool, as we'll do in this project.

NOTE: Digital artist Maggie Taylor is an expert at creating believable shadows in her work, which can be viewed at www.maggietaylor.com.

WHAT YOU'LL NEED

DIGITAL MATERIALS

Environment photo: outdoor environment that has a large ground area

Subject photo: should be holding something up, like a balloon or flag

Additional photo: balloon(s); photo with a solid background works best

Texture photo

Additional photo: for subject to hold in his/her hand

Sources for project artwork

Photo of the house:
©iStockphoto.com/shaunl

Photo of woman:
©iStockphoto.com/upheaval

Photo of balloons:
©iStockphoto.com/chieferu

Photo of suitcase:
©iStockphoto.com/nikamata

Texture: www.textureking.com

TECHNICAL SKILLS

Duplicating a file (p. 15)

Feathering (p. 16)

Moving a file into another (p. 9)

Resizing/rotating (p. 16)

Arranging layers (p. 11)

Adjusting the blending mode of a layer (p. 12)

Adjusting the Opacity of a layer (p. 12)

Adjusting Brightness/Contrast (p. 11)

Merging layers/flattening an image (p. 11)

Using Tools:

Lasso Tool (p. 9)

Magic Wand Tool (p. 9)

Eraser Tool (p. 18)

Zoom Tool (p. 18)

Crop Tool (p. 17)

Burn Tool (p. 17)

1

Select subject and place over background photo

Open the photo of the background environment, such as this house photo, and duplicate it. This will be your working file. Also open the photo of the subject. You will need a subject with his/her arm raised. (If you don't have one, stage a shoot!) This will work best with a photo of the subject holding something like a balloon or flag. In the photo, select the subject using the Magnetic Lasso Tool. Feather the edges of the selection with a Radius set to 10 pixels. Move the selection into the working file. Resize and rotate the subject as needed.

2

Clean up edges of subject

Use the Magic Wand Tool and/or Eraser Tool to clean up the edges of the subject, removing any unwanted pixels. Use the Magic Wand Tool to select unwanted areas. Adjust the Tolerance as needed—the higher the Tolerance, the more pixels will be selected. Use the Eraser Tool to erase the unwanted areas. Zoom in while erasing for the most precise work.

Select and move balloons

Open the image of the balloons. This particular image is an .eps file, which has a transparent background. This makes selecting a balloon a snap! Simply crop around the balloon you want to use, move it to the working file and resize it, and then go to EDIT>UNDO in your balloon photo. Repeat this process until the background of the working file is filled with different-sized balloons. While adding balloons to the working file, keep proportion in mind; make the balloons varying sizes so that they appear to be at different distances from the foreground.

Erase object in subject's hand

Zoom in on the object in the subject's hand. Here, my subject is holding a big balloon, which I wanted to replace with one of the other balloons. Make sure the layer of the subject is selected in the Layers Palette, and then choose the Eraser Tool. Erase the object completely. Next, add a balloon (as you did in step 3) for the subject to hold.

Add shadow to ground

To create a shadow on the ground underneath the subject, use the Burn Tool, which darkens areas of an image. Set the foreground color to black and select the Burn Tool. Adjust the Size of the tool as needed (I chose 170 pixels) and set the Range to Shadows and the Exposure to about 13%. Make sure the background environment layer is selected in the Layers Palette. Then color in a shadow on the ground beneath the subject's body. Adjust the placement of the subject as needed. (I moved the woman a bit closer to the ground so the shadow made sense.)

Add texture layer

Open the texture photo and move it into the working file. If this new layer appears behind some of the previous layers, arrange the layers so that it is in front. Set the blending mode to Color Burn and the Opacity to 52%.

Erase parts of texture layer

As needed, erase areas of the new texture layer (with the texture layer still selected). Here, I didn't like the purple hue the texture add to the woman's dress, so I erased that part of the texture layer Set the Eraser Tool Size and Opacity as desired (I set the Opacity to 52%).

Adjust Brightness/Contrast of layers

As needed, adjust the Brightness/Contrast of the layers. I increased the Brightness and Contrast of the woman to +50 and +20, respectively.

Add additional object

Add an object for the subject to hold in the other hand. Here, I added a suitcase and positioned it so the subject was letting go of it. Open the photo (one with a solid background is easiest to work with). Select the background with the Magic Wand Tool and go to SELECT>INVERSE. Move the object into the working file. Resize and rotate the new object layer as needed.

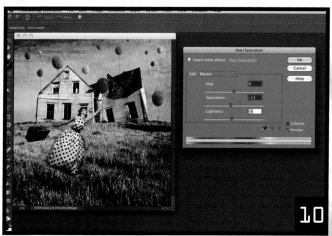

Adjust object layer

Make any desired adjustments to the Hue/Saturation and/or Brightness/Contrast of the object layer. I wanted to darken the color of my suitcase, so I adjusted the Hue/Saturation, setting the Saturation to −11 and the Lightness to −8.

■Digital Detail

Use the Blur Tool to soften the edges of layers for a more seamless transition. I did this on the edges of the suitcase and the woman.

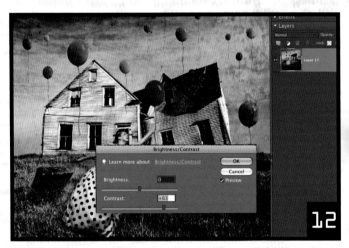

Add shadow below object

Time for more shadows! Select the background environment layer. With the Burn Tool, add a shadow beneath the object. (I took this time to also increase the shadow under the woman.) Adjust the location of the object layer (e.g., closer to the ground) if needed.

Merge layers and make final adjustments

Now that all the pieces are in place, take a look at your overall art. Is it too dull? Too colorful? Too bright? Merge all the layers, and then make adjustments using various adjustment menus as needed. I decided I wanted to dull the Saturation and increase the Contrast of my piece. I adjusted the Saturation to –62 and the Contrast to +63. When the piece is complete, flatten the image and save the file.

■Digital Detail

Learn how to create realistic-looking shadows by observing the shadows that are cast all around you in your everyday life. Take photographs of shadows cast by objects and note the light source. Study the shapes of the shadows, their direction and their intensity given the quality of light that is shining upon them.

Here's another trick for studying shadows. Take a miniature object that is similar to the object in your piece that you want to make a shadow for. Use a flashlight as your light source. I have tried this particular exercise with a dollhouse chair that I wanted to cast a spotlight on from above. I dimmed the lights and shined the flashlight on the chair from above, noting the location, shape and intensity of the shadow.

A WINTER SERENADE |

BY RICHARD SALLEY

Richard's intent in creating Winter Serenade was to suggest the soothing and warming effect of music on a winter day when one is in a pensive mood. To create the shadow of the tree, Richard made a copy of the tree and copied it to a new layer, flipped it vertically and then used the Transform Tool to elongate it. He set the blending mode of the shadow layer to Multiply and set the Opacity to 35%. A variety of blending modes and Opacity settings complete the image.

CREDITS
Software: Adobe Photoshop CS2

Technique to Try

Create a shadow of an object by duplicating the layer of the object, flipping it vertically (IMAGE>ROTATE>FLIP VERTICAL) and elongating it using the resizing function.

JUST FAMILY STOPPING BY
Replacing Parts of a Photo

I must admit that I have somewhat of a fascination with UFOs, which is something I usually keep to myself. When I was a little girl, I felt that I had experienced a close encounter, but not like the Hollywood movie kind, as it was not a frightening exchange by any means. This event made quite the impression on me and I have never forgotten the details of that night. I decided to explore that childhood memory in this piece.

In previous projects, you built upon a background photo, blending layers of elements. In addition to building layers, you can also replace areas of a background photo with other images to build an interesting montage. Here, I replaced the TV screens with a photo I created using Bryce 6.1, a 3-D modeling and animation software program. You could also replace the photo in a frame (as you did in *Walter's Broken Heart* on page 84). Other ideas include replacing a blue sky with a cloudy one or replacing grass with water or an interesting pattern. But for this project, I recommend using a photo with a television set.

WHAT YOU'LL NEED

DIGITAL MATERIALS

Environment photo: should include at least one television screen (you can add a TV image to a background photo and merge the layers to create the photo)

Additional photo: to fill the TV screen(s)

Additional photo: to be placed in the environment

Custom brush: texture brush

Sources for project artwork

Photo of scene used on TVs: on book CD

Photo of girl in field: ©iStockphoto.com/ Xaviarnau

Photo of flying saucer: ©iStockphoto.com/ Redemption

TECHNICAL SKILLS

Creating a new blank file (p. 8)

Moving a file into another (p. 9)

Arranging layers (p. 11)

Resizing/rotating (p. 16)

Adjusting Hue/Saturation (p. 12)

Selecting a foreground/ background color (p. 10)

Adjusting the Opacity of a layer (p. 12)

Merging layers/flattening an image (p. 11)

Using Tools:

Zoom Tool (p. 18)

Lasso Tool (p. 9)

Burn Tool (p. 17) (optional)

Brush Tool (p. 17)

Put environment photo in transparent file

Open the environment photo with the television set. Also create a new transparent file the same size as the photo. Make sure the Resolution is set appropriately, the Color Mode is set to RGB Color and the Background Contents are set to Transparent. Move the television photo into the blank document and center it. You can close the original photo; this new file will be your working file.

Remove TV screen

Zoom in on the television set. Use the Polygonal Lasso Tool to select the screen. (Click multiple times with your mouse as you trace around the screen to ensure that your corners are curved.) Once you have selected the screen, delete the area of the selection. You should now see the transparent background showing through the screen.

Arrange layers to fill screen

Open the photo that will fill the TV screen and move it into the working file. Arrange the layers so that the new screen layer is behind the layer with the television. The new layer should now appear through the "hole" that you have made for it in the television set. Resize it to fit the screen. Repeat this same process with other screens, as needed. Here, I used the same environment photo, but the smaller screen shows just a detail of it.

Adjust Hue/Saturation

Create a new Hue/Saturation adjustment layer. Open the menu and play with levels (the master settings and individual colors) as desired. I settled on a yellow and blue/violet contrast because I am really attracted to juxtaposing those opposites of the color wheel.

Add additional object

Open the additional photo of the object you want to add to the background. Select the object with the Magnetic Lasso Tool. Set the Feather Radius to about 10. Move it to your working file, placing and resizing it as needed.

Create shadows

At this point, add additional effects, such as shadows, if desired. Here, I added a burnt strip of ground caused by the landing/take-off of the UFO. I used the Burn Tool to create a shadow down the middle of the field. I selected a Hard Round Brush from the Default Brushes menu and set the levels of the Burn Tool as follows: Range: Shadows; Exposure: 31%; Brush Size: 371 pixels.

Stamp texture brush on new layer

Set the foreground color to black. Create a new layer, which you will use for brushwork. Then select the Brush Tool and choose a textured brush. Here, I loaded a custom brush, but you can select a textured brush, such as Texture 3 in the Assorted Brushes Menu, from the Brush Toolbar. Stamp the texture brush over the entire piece. Reduce the Opacity of the brush layer to a point where it is barely visible to achieve a subtle effect. When the piece is complete, flatten the image and save the file.

■Digital Detail

I used Bryce 6.1, a 3-D modeling and animation software program, to create the images in the TV screens. Using Bryce, you can create terrain, water, sky, rock, clouds, fog, vegetation and architecture. It also allows you to add wildlife, people, props and more to your scenes by using the DAZStudio character plug-in, which you can download for free after purchasing Bryce at www.daz3d.com/. Bryce documents are saved as .PCT files so they can be opened in Photoshop Elements.

SWEET LOLI |
BY SUSAN MCKIVERGAN

The inspiration behind Sweet Loli is an experiment with a younger Goth genre of art. Susan created Loli in the 3-D program Poser using the Fire Fly render engine. She then imported Loli into Photoshop where she built a background around her using other elements such as textures and brushwork.

CREDITS
Software: Poser 7 and Adobe Photoshop

Technique to Try
Try out a 3-D software program. (You can download a free trial of Poser 7 online.) Use your creation in a montage, applying shadows and brushwork to complete the montage.

BETWEEN WORLDS
Adding a Gradient Fill Layer for Lighting Effects

When I create art, I never feel like it comes directly from me. Instead, it comes through me from someplace greater than myself—a place that I can sense but cannot see. Thinking this way has been quite freeing, as it takes off the pressure to perform and allows me to enjoy the excitement of the creative journey. This piece is reflective of that state of being "in between worlds" when I create.

You can apply Gradient Fill Layers that utilize light modes to create a variety of lighting effects, either subtle or dramatic. For this particular piece, I used a photo of my dear friend that I staged. I extracted her figure from the photo and placed her in a new environment (part of which is a photo I took of a back road in my town). I wanted to give her a glowing, ethereal presence and was amazed at the results that were yielded by the lighting effects.

The lighting effect technique used in this project is credited to Tiffini Elektra X.

WHAT YOU'LL NEED

TECHNICAL SKILLS

Duplicating a file (p. 15)

Converting Background to Layer 0 (p. 10)

Moving a file into another (p. 9)

Resizing/rotating (p. 16)

Adjusting the blending mode of a layer (p. 12)

Adjusting the Opacity of a layer (p. 12)

Adjusting Brightness/Contrast (optional) (p. 11)

Feathering (p. 15)

Adding a Gradient Fill Layer (p. 15)

Merging layers/flattening an image (p. 11)

Using Tools:

Lasso Tool (p. 9)

Zoom Tool (p. 18)

Magic Wand Tool (p. 9)

Eraser Tool (p. 18)

DIGITAL MATERIALS

Environment photo: outdoor photo that includes the sky

Subject photo

Background photo: clouds with a color tint (such as clouds during sunset that look pink)

Additional photo (optional): texture or background

Sources for project artwork

⊙ Photo of road: on book CD

Photo of water with sun rays: ©iStockphoto.com/ rustycloud

1

Add cloud photo to environment photo
Open the environment photo and duplicate it. This will be your working file. Change the Background layer to Layer 0. Open the background photo of the tinted clouds and drag it into the working file.

2

Adjust blending mode and Opacity of cloud layer
Resize the cloud layer to fit over the background photo (Layer 0). Set the blending mode of the new layer (Layer 1) to Linear Burn, and set its Opacity to 77%. Darken the piece just a bit (and increase the contrast) to simulate nighttime, if desired.

Select and add subject

Open your subject photo and select the subject using the Magnetic Lasso Tool. Feather the edges of the selection with a Radius between 30 and 60. Move the subject into the working file. Place and resize the layer as needed.

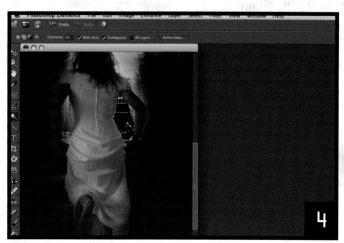

Remove unwanted areas

Remove any unwanted areas, such as those between the subject's arms and body. You can use the Magic Wand or Lasso tools to select the areas and delete them, or you can erase the areas with the Eraser Tool. Press Shift to select more than one area at a time. Zoom in for the most precise work.

Add lighting effect with Gradient Fill Layer

Now you'll give the subject a luminescent quality. Select the layer with the subject. Feather the edges of the selection with a Radius to between 30 and 60. Then add a Gradient Fill Layer (with the default settings) to produce the lighting effect. In the Layers Palette, set the fill layer's blending mode to Hard Light and Opacity to 53%.

Blend additional photos

At this point, you can add additional photos—background photos or texture photos—if desired. To highlight the subject, I added a photo of water with rays of sun shining down. I set the blending mode to Hard Light. Then I erased some of the lower half of the newest layer, revealing the brighter layers underneath. When your piece is complete, flatten the image and save the file.

THE QUIET MERMAID | BY TIFFINI ELEKTRA X

Tiffini created digital illustrations of the mermaid and sea horse in Illustrator. Then she brought them into Photoshop, where she applied a Gradient Fill Layer to both the entire piece and to sections of the piece.

CREDITS
Software: Adobe Photoshop CS4, Adobe Illustrator CS4

Technique to Try
Create a digital collage or montage incorporating an illustration along with photos. Apply a Gradient Fill Layer to part of the piece.

WINTER
Using Staged Photos

As you know by now, the key to a montage is using images that fit together to form a believable whole. One easy way to ensure a subject photo that fits your needs is to stage your own photo shoot. In addition, it allows you to include a photo that is personal, with deep meaning to you. In her book, *Altered Imagery*, Karen Michel talks about the power of using our own imagery in our artwork. She says, "Every photograph represents a part of our personal history: places we have been or people we have known and who are special in our life. Rather than using a picture of a stranger ... we can include one of a friend or family member and merge memory with our art."

I could not agree more. This particular piece utilizes a photo I staged with a dear friend. As I worked with my friend's likeness, I was astounded by the amount of emotional attachment I felt to the work. My love for my friend wove its way through my artistic process, influencing every artistic choice and infusing each decision and element with authenticity and deep personal meaning. I never had a favorite piece that I created ... up until this point.

WHAT YOU'LL NEED

DIGITAL MATERIALS

Subject photo: this will be staged in step 1

Environment photos: two related nature photos, such as snow-covered trees and an icy field

Additional photos: to add to the subject photo, such as wings

Texture photos: one with tint of color, a natural texture and one additional

Sources for project artwork

○ Photo of frosty field: on book CD
○ Photo of trees: on book CD

Photo of dove: ©iStockphoto.com/xyno

Photo of wing: ©iStockphoto.com/Grafissimo

Concrete texture: www.textureking.com

TECHNICAL SKILLS

Creating a new blank file (p. 8)

Moving a file into another (p. 9)

Resizing/rotating (p. 16)

Adjusting the blending mode of a layer (p. 12)

Arranging layers (p. 10)

Adjusting the Opacity of a layer (p. 12)

Feathering (p. 16)

Using Tools:

　Eraser Tool (p. 18)

　Zoom Tool (p. 18)

　Magic Wand Tool (p. 9)

　Lasso Tool (p. 9)

　Brush Tool (p. 17)

Stage subject photo

Before you begin, take your staged subject photo. Think about what you want the subject to be doing in your piece, and pose your model appropriately. For my piece, I wanted the subject to hold a dove, so I staged a photo with my friend posing with her hand out. The background in your staged photo doesn't matter since you will be selecting just the subject.

Add environment to transparent working file

Create a new file approximately 8" × 10" (20cm × 25cm) at 300 dpi with Color Mode set to RGB color, and Background Contents set to Transparent. This will be your working file. Open one of the background photos of nature. (Here, the theme of my piece is winter, so I chose wintry photos.) Move the photo to your working file. Resize it as needed to fit the file.

Add second environment photo and adjust layer

Open the photo of the second environment. Move it into your working file and resize it to fit. Set the blending mode of this new layer (Layer 3) to Darken.

Erase top environment layer

Zoom in on the middle of the working file, and use the Eraser Tool to scrub away some of the top environment layer to reveal more of the layer underneath. Set the Opacity of the Eraser to about 45%.

Select and add subject

Open the staged subject photo and use the Magnetic Lasso Tool to select the subject. Feather the edges using a Radius set to 10. Move the selection into the working file and resize the layer as needed.

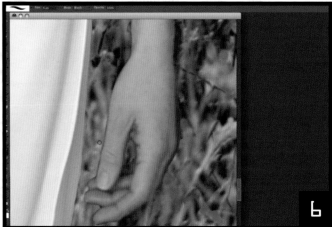

Clean edges of subject layer

Remove any unwanted areas around the edges of the selection. You can use the Magic Wand or Lasso tools to select the areas and delete them, or you can erase the areas with the Eraser Tool. Zoom in on the layer to achieve the most precise work.

Make adjustments to staged subject

Make adjustments to the subject as needed. Here, I colorized the woman's hair red using the Brush Tool. I set the foreground color to red and chose a Soft Round Brush from the Default Brushes Menu in the Brush Toolbar. I changed the Opacity of the brush to 59%.

Add first element to subject

Now you'll add elements to your staged subject. I added wings and a dove. To add the first wing, I opened a photo of a wing on a white background. Using the Magic Wand Tool, I selected the white background and inverted the selection (SELECT>INVERT). I moved it into the working file and placed it by the woman, resizing and rotating it. I moved the wing behind the woman by arranging the layers.

Continue adding elements

To add the other wing, I went back to the image of the wing and flipped it by going to IMAGE>ROTATE>FLIP HORIZONTAL. Once it was in the working file, I adjusted the placement, size and rotation of both wings so that they look like a pair.

Add elements without solid backgrounds

If an element does not have a solid background, select it in the photo with the Magnetic Lasso Tool and feather the edges with a Radius of 10. Move the selection into the working file, and place and resize it as needed. Use the Magic Wand Tool and/or Eraser Tool to clean up the edges of the selection.

11

Add tinted texture layer

Open the tinted texture photo. Move the image to the working file and resize it to fit. Make sure this new layer is in front. Set the blending mode of this layer to Color Dodge and the Opacity to 58%.

12

Add natural texture layer

Open the natural texture photo and move it to the working file. Resize it as needed to fit the working file, and make sure the layer is in front. Set the blending mode to Multiply and Opacity to 80%. Select the Eraser Tool and set it to a Soft Round Brush, Size at about 90 pixels and Opacity about 20%. Then erase parts of the natural texture layer that cover up the subject.

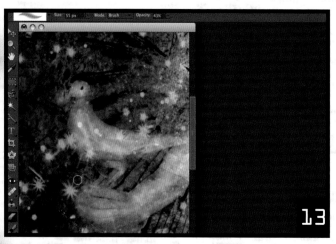

13

Add last texture photo

Open the remaining texture photo and move it into the working file. Here, I added a photo of twinkling lights. Resize the layer as needed. Set the blending mode to Lighten and the Opacity to about 50%. Erase parts of the texture photo as needed. I set the Eraser Tool to Soft Round Brush, with a Size of about 55 pixels and Opacity about 55%. When the piece is complete, flatten the image and save the file.

■Digital Detail

As this piece was deeply personal for me, I tried to use my own photos for the montage. All images are mine except for the dove and wings. Oh, how I desperately wanted to use my own photo of a bird wing. But bird wings aren't easy to come by, nor did I think I had the stomach to handle finding one! Thank goodness for iStockphoto.

You'll find that many of the projects in this book include photos from www.istock-photo.com. The site has a massive collection of royalty free images. The photos aren't free, but they're inexpensive, especially if you just need a background for adding texture, which can be a low resolution. Low-resolution photos can be as inexpensive as $1. In addition to iStockphoto, be sure to check out these other stock photo sites:
www.morguefile.com
www.imagecatalog.com

A SERIES OF MINOR DISTRACTIONS |

BY MIKEL ROBINSON

A Series of Minor Distractions *is a piece, as the name suggests, that speaks to how easy it is to focus on the small problems in our lives at the expense of missing the larger picture.*

Staged subject photos aren't the only personal images that make for great montages. Scanned elements also provide wonderful imagery. Mikel used a variety of scanned elements to create this piece. Scanned items include an old glass plate negative of a man, a 19th century egg engraving and a pocket watch face, along with scanned photographs of a pocket watch, a crow, a tree and a run-down house near where Mikel lives.

CREDITS
Software: Adobe Photoshop CS2

Technique to Try

Scan some objects—book pages, old letters, found objects, leaves, etc.—and incorporate them into a digital montage.

5

Altering Art

Incorporating traditional art into digital works

There is a collage I created a few years ago—an elderly woman, clad in a babushka and jeans with pink polka dots, hunched over a canvas, painting away to her heart's content. I want that to be me one day, still curious, childlike and passionate about art. That is why I so loved this collage (which you can see in step 1 on page 123). There was one problem, however: some of the design elements didn't work. I wasn't sure how to rework the piece without destroying some of the elements that I adored. So, I kept the collage on a shelf in my studio where it could catch my eye each day. I kept hoping for that "aha" moment. One day, I walked by and it dawned on me what I needed to do.

With the tools in Photoshop Elements, I was able to alter the collage, taking out the elements I did not like and enhancing the ones I did. What I learned is to hold on to those pieces that speak to you but don't feel like they are complete yet. You can alter them! And don't stop at altering just a single piece of art. Use your work as backgrounds in montages, and blend multiple works of art in a collage. Or deconstruct a piece and reconstruct it on a whole new level. You really can alter your art in so many ways—and blend your first love of traditional art with this newfound digital enjoyment.

As I mentioned, I created this collage a few years ago, and loved it at the time because of what it symbolized. I wish to be vibrant, able and curious in my old age. I subscribe to the sentiment that it is never too late to learn something new, and, in that vein, I hope to be a lifelong learner.

Pieces of that collage however, made me cringe. Like the big, rectangular swatch of yellow in the background—what is that? And those bold white strokes around her figure? What was I thinking? I know we all feel this way at times when reflecting on our artwork. The cool thing about Photoshop Elements is that you can scan these pieces of "actual" art onto your computer and alter them with the program, bringing them to a place that "works." I'm sure I will want to tweak this work again a few more years from now, when I know more. The beauty is that you can readily do this without destroying key elements of the piece that you want to keep intact.

WHAT YOU'LL NEED

DIGITAL MATERIALS

- Scan of original art
- Texture photos (at least two)

Sources for project artwork

Photo of multi-colored texture: WHEREISWHERE (www.flickr.com/groups/textures4layers)

Photo of yellow texture: Eddi 07 (www.flickr.com/groups/textures4layers)

TECHNICAL SKILLS

Adjusting Hue/Saturation (p. 12)

Moving a file into another (p. 9)

Resizing/rotating (p. 16)

Adjusting the Opacity of a layer (p. 12)

Adjusting the blending mode of a layer (p. 12)

Merging layers/flattening an image (p. 11)

Adjusting Color Curves (p. 11)

Using Tools:

Lasso Tool (p. 9)

Eraser Tool (p. 18)

Crop Tool (p. 17) (optional)

Clone Stamp Tool (p. 17)

Scan art and open file

Scan your piece of original art and open the file. This will be your working file.

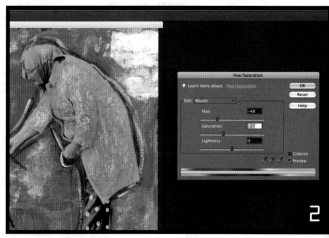

Adjust colors

Adjust the Hue/Saturation of the piece. I altered the colors of the entire piece, setting the Hue to −48 and Saturation to −27. If you prefer, you can alter the colors of just one area. To do this, select the area with the Lasso Tool first, then go to the Hue/Saturation Menu. You can also alter select tones by changing Edit in the menu.

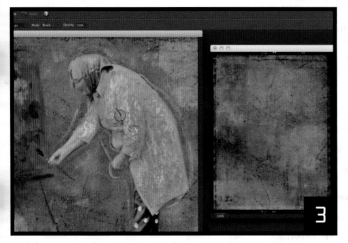

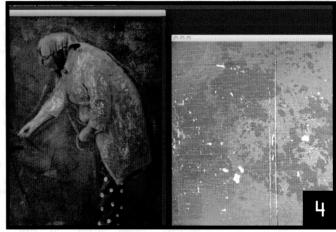

Add texture layer to mask areas

To mask some of the less-than-satisfactory areas of your piece, add a texture layer. Open the texture photo and move it into your working file. Resize it as needed. Use the Eraser Tool to erase the parts of the texture layer that cover up areas of your piece you want to remain exposed. I erased over the subject in my piece. Adjust the Opacity of the layer, as desired. I set mine to 68%. I also cropped the image just a bit.

Add more textures

Continue adding texture layers to create richness and depth. I moved a yellow-tinted texture layer into my working file. I set the blending mode to Color Burn and the Opacity to 57%. This produced a warm, glowing appearance. Then I added a blue-tinted texture layer. I set the blending mode to Overlay and the Opacity to 12%.

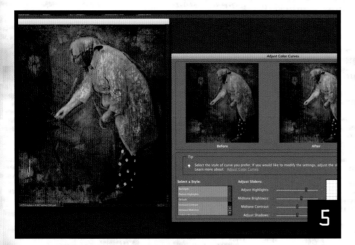

Merge layers and adjust lighting

Merge the layers. To adjust the lighting of your piece, open the Adjust Color Curves Menu. I chose Default and increased both the Highlights and the Brightness.

Make final adjustments

Make any final adjustments, such as removing unwanted marks (like the white lines I removed around my subject). To remove marks, use the Clone Stamp Tool to replace the marks with parts of the background. When you're finished, save the file.

EMILY DICKINSON |
BY PENELOPE DULLAGHAN

Penelope created her piece as a traditional painting using acrylic paint on paper. She then scanned the work into Photoshop to correct color and add elements like the red grasses. In Photoshop, color is corrected using the Color Curves and Hue/ Saturation manipulations.

CREDITS
Software: Adobe Photoshop CS3

Technique to Try
Use just the adjustment menus (e.g., Brightness/ Contrast, Hue/Saturation) to enhance a piece of art.

CELIE

Using Art as a Background

I'll never forget the movie *The Color Purple*. One moment will stay with me forever: the heartrending scene where Celie is torn from her sister Nettie, sold to be the wife of a man she doesn't know. I have always remembered Celie, and this piece is my ode to her.

I have a passion for creating painted backgrounds. When I first started creating mixed-media art I made mostly artist trading cards. I would start by creating a background in which to place my designs. My favorite part of creating the ATC, by far, was creating these backgrounds made of layers of paint, paper, ink, scratches and more paint. Even though my primary focus is on digital art and photography these days, I thoroughly enjoy making painted backgrounds that I can incorporate into digital work, as I did for this project.

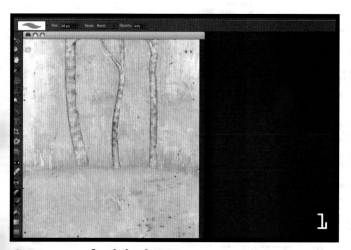

Open scan of original art

Open the file with the scan of original art. This will be your working file. I created an illustrated background piece in my studio for the purpose of adding a subject digitally.

Add environment photo

Open the environment photo and move it to your working file. Position the layer as desired. I added a flower field photo to my piece and placed it to cover the background's painted grass.

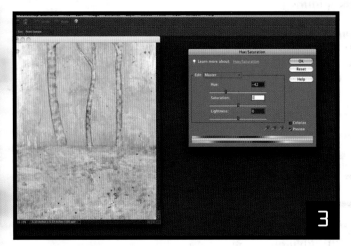

Adjust layer to match background

Set the blending mode of the new layer to Soft Light. Adjust the color in the Hue/Saturation Menu to blend with the illustrated environment.

Soften edges to blend

Soften the edge of the newest layer to blend it. Use the Eraser Tool set to an Opacity of about 45% and erase over the edges.

Add subject layer

Open the subject photo and select the subject using the Magnetic Lasso Tool. Move the selection to the working file, and resize the layer as needed. Arrange the layers so that the subject layer is behind the environment photo. This will allow the subject to appear as if he/she is standing in the middle of the environment (here, amongst the flowers).

Erase unwanted areas

Zoom in on the subject and use the Eraser Tool and/or Magic Wand Tool to remove any unwanted pixels around the edge. Adjust the Size and Opacity of the tools as necessary. Then select the environment layer. With the Eraser Tool set to an Opacity of 80%, erase the parts of the layer that cover up everything above the subject's knees. Here, I erased the flowers and field that covered the child's dress and hands.

Add drop shadow to subject

Select the layer with the subject. Go to the Effects Palette and select the Layer Styles icon. Select Drop Shadows from the drop-down menu, and choose the Soft Edge shadow (click then apply). You can adjust the shadow as desired by clicking on the "fx" icon in that layer in the Layers Palette.

Add additional photo layer

Open the additional photo. Select the object and move it into the working file. Adjust the size, placement and edges as needed. I added a butterfly to my piece, rotating and resizing it smaller to make sense next to the subject.

Adjust color of new layer to coordinate

Adjust the Hue/Saturation of the additional photo layer to coordinate with the background. I set the Hue to –119, Saturation to –2 and Lightness to +54.

■ Digital Detail

Observant readers will notice the butterfly in step 8 looks a bit familiar. Yes, that's the same butterfly I used in The Chase *(on page 96). But you'll notice that after the Hue/Saturation adjustments are made to the butterfly layer in step 9, it looks like a completely different image.*

Don't think you have to go out and buy new photos, brushes and texture for each project you create. The great thing about digital elements is that you can re-use them as many times as you like. And with the various tools in Photoshop Elements you can alter an image to fit with multiple pieces. Try altering the color of a digital scrapbook paper and see how it changes. Add a filter to a stock photo. Increase the contrast of a texture. Play around and have fun!

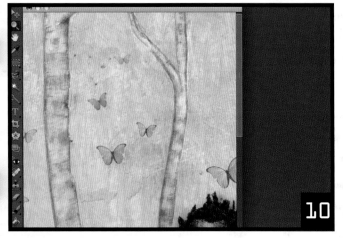

Duplicate the additional photo layer
Duplicate the layer of the additional photo. Move, resize and rotate the layer as needed. Repeat the process to add multiple objects to the background. For more depth, adjust the Hue/Saturation of some of the layers.

Add vintage texture layer
Open the vintage texture photo and move it into the working file. Resize it as needed to fit the file. Set this layer's blending mode to Multiply and its Opacity to 36%.

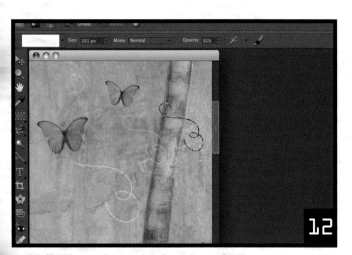

Add final touches with brushwork
Add final touches with brushwork. I used a swirly glitter brush to create subtle signs of movement beneath the butterflies. Add the brushwork on a new layer and adjust the Opacity of this new layer as desired. When you're finished, flatten the image and save the file.

MASKED |
BY IZABELLA PIERCE

"It was 3 a.m.," Izabella shares. *"I awoke from an eerie dream and went to my library to read some poetry. I opened the book to 'The Mask' by William Butler Yeats. After reading the poem, I was greatly inspired to create."*

Izabella enjoys giving her work a distressed and vintage quality by adding layers that are grungy and scratchy in style, as she did in this piece. As you saw in step 3 of the main project, the Soft Light blending mode works very well to blend layers. In this piece, Izabella applied the Soft Light blending mode (among others) and scaled down the Opacity of the layers to about 85%.

CREDITS
Software: Adobe Photoshop CS2
Other elements: Enchanted Merchantile CD

Technique to Try
Blend an illustrated background with at least five other layers. Apply the Soft Light blending mode with varying opacities to the layers.

THE RHYTHM
Deconstructing and Reconstructing Art

Have you ever created art where you really love aspects of the piece, but the composition as a whole is off? We are all nodding. One of these "off" pieces sat in my studio for a few months. I'd pick it up, stare at it and prepare to slab some paint on. For some reason, I continued to put it down, until one day I came across an idea by Sarah Fishburn where you take a collage, tear it apart digitally and put it back together in a new form. This technique can help you take those compositions that have gone awry and give them a sense of balance and new life, just like it did with my wayward piece featured in this project.

WHAT YOU'LL NEED

TECHNICAL SKILLS

Creating a new blank file (p. 8)

Moving a file into another (p. 9)

Resizing/rotating (p. 16)

Adjusting the Opacity of a layer (p. 12)

Merging layers/flattening an image (p. 11)

Feathering (p. 16)

Adjusting the blending mode of a layer (p. 12)

Using Tools:

Lasso Tool (p. 9)

Marquee Tool (p. 18)

Eraser Tool (p. 18)

Crop Tool (p. 17)

DIGITAL MATERIALS

Scan of original art

Texture photo: tinted similar in tone to original art

Sources for project artwork

Blue texture photo: a travers les blumes (www.flickr.com/groups/textures4layers)

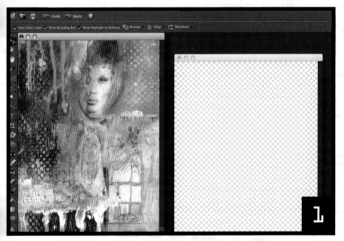

1

Open original art file and create new file
Open the file with the scan of your art. Then create a new blank document. Make this new file the same size as your original art file. Set the Color Mode of the new file to RGB Color and the Background Contents to Transparent. This will be your working file.

2

Move part of original art to working file
Now you'll add parts of the original art file to the transparent file. Go to the original art file and use the Lasso Tool or Marquee Tool to select a part of the piece. Move the selection to the working file.

Continue adding parts of original art

Go back to the original art file and move another selection to the working file. Repeat to add additional parts to the working file. Experiment with resizing and rotating selections. When finished, merge the layers.

Duplicate part of new collage

Choose a part of the working file to duplicate. I decided I wanted to make the head more of a focal point. Select the area with the Lasso Tool and feather the edges of the selection with a Radius of 10 pixels. Duplicate the selection by going to EDIT>COPY and then EDIT>PASTE. Move the new layer and resize/rotate it as needed.

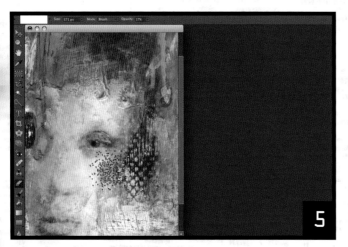

Blend and rough up edges

Soften the edges of the duplicated layer with the Eraser Tool to blend it with the rest of the piece. Set the Eraser Tool to a Soft Round Brush and reduce the Opacity. Erase the edges of the layer. To give the selection a roughed-up look, change the Eraser Tool and erase the edges again. This time, choose the Dry Brush Tip Light Flow Brush (from the Default Brushes drop-down menu). Set the brush to a larger size and lower the Opacity (to less than 20%).

Add tinted texture photo

Open the tinted texture photo (I used one in a dark blue) and move it to your working file. Resize the layer as needed to fit the file. Then set the layer's blending mode to Overlay.

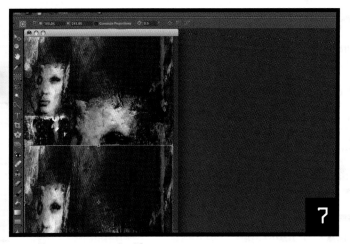

Duplicate upper half

Merge the layers. With the Rectangular Marquee Tool, select the upper half of your piece. Copy and paste it as you did in step 4. Then move the duplicated section down, covering the lower half completely.

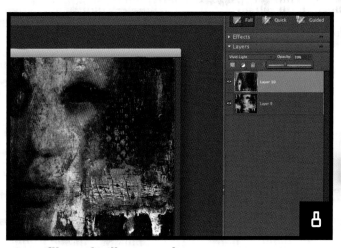

Crop file and adjust new layer

Crop the piece to remove the upper half. Then set the blending mode of the newest layer to Vivid Light and Opacity to 39%. This will reveal the layer beneath with altered tonal values. Flatten and save the file.

RETROSPECTIVE | BY SARAH FISHBURN

Sarah scanned her painted collage to deconstruct it using Adobe Photoshop. She says, "Simple Photoshop effects can provide a lot of impact with judicious application." She manipulated colors and enhanced the Brightness/Contrast. She also used the Marquee Tool to selectively cut and reposition sections, which she then resized and rotated, creating a digital mosaic.

CREDITS
Software: Adobe Photoshop CS3

Technique to Try
Create a collage for the purpose of deconstructing it. Don't think as you work—just create! Then see what you can re-create in Photoshop Elements using pieces of the collage.

INSPIRATION

THE POWER OF PRAYER
Blending Multiple Works of Art

I created this piece during a time when so many people around me were facing incredibly hard life challenges, most of them in the form of serious illness. I found myself sending many prayers out into the universe for strength, healing and hope. This piece is a manifestation of my state of mind at that time.

I constructed the main elements of design for this piece from multiple pieces of art: a painted background, a portion of a collage (the close-up face of a woman) and a digitally altered vintage photo. Go through your own artwork, find elements that appeal to you, scan them into your computer and follow the proverbial muse to find creative ways to combine them into one cohesive design.

Technique credited to Pilar Isabel Pollock

WHAT YOU'LL NEED

DIGITAL MATERIALS

Scans of original art: background and additional

Custom brush (optional): grunge brush

Background photo: graffiti wall

Additional photo: of a subject

Font

Sources for project artwork
Photo of graffiti: www.morguefile.com

Font: 1942 Report font (www.dafont.com)

TECHNICAL SKILLS

Converting Background to Layer 0 (p. 10)

Applying the Invert Filter (p. 14)

Creating a new layer (p. 10)

Loading a custom brush (p. 16) (optional)

Adjusting the blending mode of a layer (p. 12)

Adjusting the Opacity of a layer (p. 12)

Moving a file to another/moving a layer (p. 9)

Resizing/rotating (p. 16)

Merging layers/flattening an image (p. 11)

Feathering (p. 16)

Using Tools:

Eyedropper Tool (p. 18)

Brush/Pencil Tool (p. 17)

Magic Wand Tool (p. 9)

Lasso Tool (p. 9)

Type Tool (p. 18)

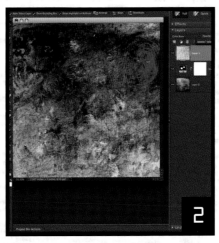

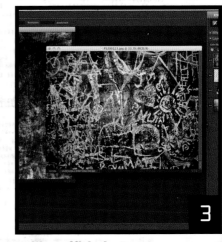

Apply Invert Filter
Open the file with the original art background. This will be your working file. Change the Background layer to Layer 0. Then apply the Invert Filter on a new adjustment layer.

Stamp grunge brush
Create a new layer. Select one of the darker colors in your piece using the Eyedropper Tool. (This will set the foreground color.) Then select the Brush Tool and choose the grunge brush. (You can load a custom brush or use one of the program's textured brushes. I chose a custom scratch brush.) Set the blending mode of the new layer to Color Burn and lower the Opacity. I set mine to 32%.

Add graffiti photo
Open the photo of the graffiti wall and move it to the working file. Resize this new layer to fit the working file. Set the blending mode to Color Burn and lower the Opacity level. I set mine to 39%.

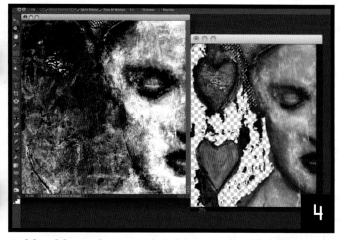

Add subject photo and delete parts of layer

Open the file with the scan of additional art. (I scanned one of my journal covers.) Use the Magic Wand Tool set to a Tolerance of 50 to randomly select and delete parts of the image. Then move it into the working file, and resize it as needed.

Add additional photo and alter layer

Merge all the layers. Then open the additional photo of the person. I used a vintage Communion photo of a girl that I'd previously altered. Select the subject/object in the additional photo with the Magnetic Lasso Tool, and feather the edges with a Radius of about 30 pixels. Move the selection into the working file and set the blending mode of the layer to Difference. Then use the Magic Wand Tool set to a Tolerance of 50 to randomly select and delete parts of this new layer.

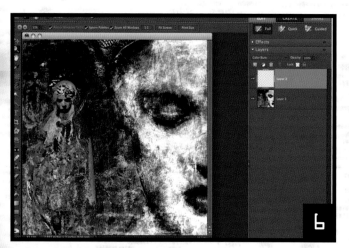

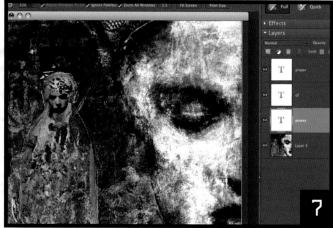

Add additional brushwork

Merge all the layers. Add more grunge brush marks in tones that match the additional photo layer. I wanted to warm the piece up a bit to better accommodate the yellow tones of the girl, so I stamped in yellow paint with my custom grunge brush on a new layer. Set the blending mode of your new brush layer to Color Burn. If desired, use the Pencil Tool set to a Hard Round Brush at 1 pixel to trace around the additional photo layer. Put this pencil work on a new layer. Then merge the layers.

Add text layers

With the Type Tool, add text to the piece. Put each word on its own layer so that they can be moved and changed individually. I typed the words *power of prayer* on different layers. Adjust the Opacity of each text layer, if desired. When you're finished, flatten the image and save the file.

PUNK'D | BY PILAR
ISABEL POLLOCK

For this piece, Pilar wanted to portray the grit and grunge of the eighties underground punk movement, but with a modern edge. To start, she inverted a hand-painted journal page using Photoshop Elements. She stamped with digital brushes and added several textural image layers and Color Fill Layers. Pilar applied the Color Burn blending mode to both the texture layer and Color Fill Layer. The texture layers consisted of scans of tea-stained material, alcohol-dyed transparencies, burned material and photographs from a salvage yard.

CREDITS
Software: Adobe Photoshop Elements 6.0
1976 Digital Stamps: by meth
(http://meth.deviantart.com)

Technique to Try
Scan your own texture backgrounds and use those in a piece. Apply the Invert Filter to at least one of the backgrounds.

DIGITAL SHOWCASE

This gallery contains works that I created using combinations of the techniques featured in this book. I encourage you to do the same, combining techniques in new and interesting ways to yield complex pieces rich in color, value, design and texture.

DANCE ON

I am a flutist, so I know what it feels like to have stage fright. Miraculously, I have always found a way to push through, as performers do. We dance on, transcend those feelings of self-doubt and fear, and can truly fly if we choose to let go and enjoy the ride. Dance On is an exploration and visual representation of stage fright.

CREDITS
Stage: ©iStockphoto.com/billyfoto; spilled milk: ©iStockphoto.com/marykan; water: by seemann (www.morguefile.com); ballerina: Lori Vrba (www.lorivrba.com)

Techniques Include
Creating a spotlight effect with the Gradient Fill Layer; creating shadows with the Burn Tool; colorizing imagery with the Brush Tool; applying the Poster Edges Filter; applying a Solid Color Fill Layer (brown with a very low Opacity); applying a Color Burn blending mode

LOVE POTION NUMBER 9

This piece was inspired by the famous oldie "Love Potion No. 9." I attempted to capture that lovesick feeling we have all had at one time or another. It looks like the subject of my piece took a big swig from that love juice bottle on the floor.

CREDITS
Chair: ©iStockphoto.com/sswartz; forest: ©iStockphoto.com/contour99; heart bottle: earl53 (www.morguefile.com); lightning brush (www.obsidiandawn.com)

Techniques Include
Creating a spotlight effect using the Lighting Effects Filter; creating shadows with the Burn Tool; applying a Solid Color Fill Layer; adjusting Brightness/Contrast levels; applying blending modes and adjusting their Opacity levels; duplicating layers and applying blending modes to them

HOME SWEET HOME

I am obsessed with candy and have a secret sweet stash drawer in my studio, taking up precious art supply space. Candy makes me happy. What better way to celebrate my sweet tooth than by creating a digital homestead made of candy?

CREDITS
Candy cane: ©iStockphoto.com/DNY59; cupcake: ©iStockphoto.com/subjug; M&M's: ©iStockphoto.com/phottoman; gumdrops: ©iStockphoto.com/arcimages; lollipops: ©iStockphoto.com/Sonus; heart cookie: ©iStockphoto.com/myadria; house: jusben at www.morguefile.com; field: bosela at www.morguefile.com; girl: nemo65 at Vintage Photo Sharing group on Flickr

Techniques Include
Selecting objects with the Magnetic Lasso Tool and cleaning the edges with the Eraser Tool; adding texture photos and adjusting the blending modes (Saturation, Color Burn and Overlay) and Opacity levels

HEART TETHERED TO UP

I've often dreamed about what it might be like to fly freely over my town, marveling at the tiny farmhouses, fields, woods and rivers below. I made my flight of fancy come true through the magic of digital art. If you look closely, you can make out actual imagery of homes and landscape from the town in which I live.

CREDITS
Balloon (www.morguefile.com)

Techniques Include
Creating a shadow effect with a Solid Color Fill Layer of black and a reduced Opacity; applying blending modes to layers and adjusting their Opacity levels

INDEX

Adjust Smart Fix, 12, 45

Altered Imagery, 115

Art, original, 7

    altering/enhancing, 121–125

    using as background, 126–131

    blending multiple works, 136–139

    enhancing, 122–125

    reconstructing, 132–135

    traditional, 39–41, 44–49

Blending Modes, 10, 12–14, 140–141

Brightness/Contrast, 11, 140

Brown, Chris, 33

Brush toolbar, 48. *See also* Custom
    brushes

Brushwork, 39, 45–46, 130

Bryce 6.1, 109

Cole, Shona, 41

Collage, digital, 7, 63–89, 91, 121

    self-portrait, 80–83

Colors, 10–14

    inverting, 16

    popping areas of, 26–29

Color Curves, 11, 66, 123

Cullimore, Sonya, 25, 29

Custom brushes, 19, 32, 45–47, 59

    creating, 92–95

    loading, 16, 137

Daguerreotypes, 21, 51

Deconstruction, 132–135

Deselecting, 10

Drop Shadows, 47, 87

Dullaghan, Penelope, 125

Effects Palette, 14–15, 32, 127

Elektra X, Tiffani, 99, 111, 113

Feathering, 16, 24, 112, 133, 137

Files

    creating and saving, 8–9

    duplicating, 15

    JPEG and TIFF files, 9

    working, 8

Filters, 14–15, 39

    Artistic Filters, drawing with, 40–43

    Blur Filter, 15, 17, 96–99

        creating shadows with, 100–105

    Colored Pencil Filter, 14, 40–43

    Dry Brush Filter, 14, 40, 42–43

    Gaussian Blur Filter, 14, 28, 53, 98

    Invert Filter, 14, 68–70

    Lighting Effects Filter, 13–14,
        72–75, 110–113, 140

    Liquefy Filter, 48

    Motion Blur Filter, 14, 97

    Photo Filter, 15, 72–75

    Poster Edges Filter, 15, 68–70, 140

    Texturizer Filter, 60

    Watercolor Filter, 40

Fishburn, Sarah, 133, 135

Fonts, 19, 30

Gaynor, Sheri, 43

Gordon, Susanna, 55

Graminski, Peggi Mayer, 71

Graphics tablet, 8–9

Highlights, 12, 65–66

Haun, Gregory, 7, 91

Hue/Saturation, 12–13, 48, 53–54,
    66, 123, 127

Hydeck, Chrysti, 36–37

Images

    adjusting, 11–12

    resizing, 8, 16

    rotating and flipping, 16

Layers, 10–11, 17, 58, 63, 86

    arranging, 11

    background, 10

    blending, 12–14

    creating new, 8, 137

    duplicating, 10–11, 127, 140

    Fill Layers, 15

        Gradient Fill Layer, 15, 110–113,
        140

        Solid Color Fill Layer, 15, 22–25,
        50–55, 140–141

    merging, 11, 64–67, 104

    of paint, 56

resizing, 16

rotating/flipping, 16

of text, 32

textural, 21

transparent, 64–67

Masking technique, 89

Materials, 8

McKivergan, Susan, 61, 109

Michel, Karen, 115

Montage art, digital, 7, 91

Motion, producing, 96–99

Opacity, 10, 12, 56, 140–141

Otero, Marie, 67

Paint colors, 10

Paintings, 7, 39, 44–49. *See also* Art

Photomanipulation, 7, 21

Photopainting, 57

Photos, 19

   background, 19, 69, 97, 101, 118

   colorizing, 21, 84–89, 140

   environment, 19, 94, 107, 111,
      115–116, 127

   focal point of, 23

   graffiti, 137

   painting, 7, 56–61

   portrait, 51–54

   replacing parts of, 106–109

   staging, 114–119

subject, 19, 69, 74, 94, 115

texture, 19, 35–36, 54, 66, 70, 74,
   82, 141

   tinting, 50–55, 84–89

   vintage, 84

Photoshop Collage Techniques, 7, 91

Pierce, Izabella, 131

Pollock, Pilar Isabel, 139

Portraits, 51–54

Printing, 8–9, 47

Resolution, 8

Robinson, Mikel, 119

Salley, Richard, 89, 105

Saturation, 12–13, 48, 53–54, 66

Scrapbook kits, 76–79

Scrapbooks, digital, 7, 63

Shadows, 12, 100–105, 108, 140–141

Shadows/Highlights, 12, 65–66

Sharpness, adjusting, 12, 32

Shefveland, Michelle, 79

Sheridan, Kelly, 49, 95

Spotlight effect, 140

Style menu, 32

Taylor, Maggie, 101

Texture, overlaying, 34–37

Tools, 8–18

   Blur Tool, 101–103

   Brush/Pencil Tool, 17–18, 39, 48, 140.

   See also Custom brushes

   colorizing with, 84–89

   Burn/Dodge Tool, 17, 140

   Clone Stamp Tool, 17, 60, 82

   Color Replacement Tool, 17

   Crop Tool, 17, 36

   Elliptical Marquee Tool, 23

   Eraser Tool, 18, 24, 141

   Eyedropper Tool, 18

   Lasso Tool, 9–10

   Magic Wand Tool, 9

   Magnetic Lasso Tool, 9, 141

   Marquee Tool, 18

   Move Tool, 9

   Paint Bucket Tool, 18

   Polygonal Lasso Tool, 10

   Type Tool, 18, 31–33

   Zoom Tool, 18

Type, designing with, 30–33, 78

van der Werf, Julia, 83

Vignettes, creating, 21–25

Web sources

   for custom brushes, 44

   for digital scrapbook kits, 78

   for fonts, 30

   for stock photos, 118

   for texture photos, 36

Express your creativity
with these other titles from F+W Media.

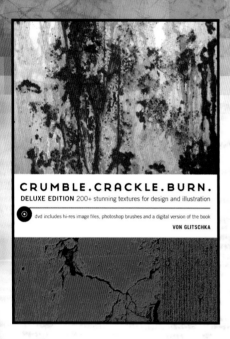

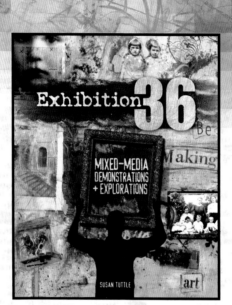

Crumble, Crackle, Burn: Deluxe Edition
Von Glitschka

Crumble, Crackle, Burn: Deluxe Edition *is an affordable tool for transforming your images with textures—you'll find 228 royalty-free textures you can use in your digital artwork. The book features 168 textures with beautiful full-color examples of how each texture can be used. Plus, the included DVD contains an additional 60 textures.*

ISBN 10: 1-60061-798-0
ISBN 13: 978-1-60061-798-0
hardcover + DVD, 128 pages, Z5258

Exhibition 36
Susan Tuttle

Inside Exhibition 36, *you'll enter a virtual gallery featuring the work of thirty-six mixed-media artists. Each artist is "present" in his or her exhibit, answering questions, sharing thoughts, talking about the work and offering instruction. As a bonus, you'll find imagery contributed by the artists for you to reuse in your own creations.*

ISBN-10: 1-60061-104-4
ISBN-13: 978-1-60061-104-9
paperback, 160 pages, Z2065

Image Transfer Workshop
Darlene Olivia McElroy and Sandra Duran Wilson

Learn 35 transfer techniques that cover everything from basic tape and gel medium transfers to much more advanced techniques. Image Transfer Workshop *provides a quick reference and examples of art using a variety of techniques that will inspire you to go beyond single transfer applications. Troubleshooting fixes will even enable you to work with your transfers that don't quite live up to expectations.*

ISBN-10: 1-60061-160-5
ISBN-13: 978-1-60061-160-5
paperback, 128 pages, Z2509

These and other fine F+W Media titles are available at your local craft retailer, bookstore or online supplier, or visit our Web site at www.mycraftivitystore.com.